Discourse Markers Decoded:
The Art of Clear and
Effective Communication

意見·主張を
クリアに
伝える技術

ディスコース
マーカーで
英語はこんなに
伝わる

無料音声
ダウンロード付

コチェフ アレクサンダー·著

JN057410

ベレ出版

Start!

はじめに

一般的に言語を学ぶには、読む・聞く・書く・話すの「四技能」が必要と言われています。理想的な言語習得は、四技能が等しく少しずつ伸びていくことだと言っても良いでしょう。しかし実際に学んでいく中で、どうしても読む・聞くのインプットスキルに比べて書く・話すのアウトプットスキルが思うように成長しないなと感じる方は多いのではないでしょうか。その理由に関して、「話す機会が少ない」「文法を意識し過ぎ」など様々な説明がなされますが、そういった犯人捜しのような評論的なスタンスにはさほど有用性や魅力を私は感じません。教える現場から発想する、リアルに効いて、即効性のあるソリューションをたくさん提供していけば、学習者のレベルアップに確実に貢献できると思うからです。

この本は、英語を教える現場でアウトプットスキルの強化を念頭に生まれたひとつのソリューションです。ビジネスパーソン、大学生、大学院生、大学教員、公務員など様々な学習者の弱いところを分析して、効果の高い、即効性のある学びを提供するために内容を組み立てました。

3冊の著書に加え、制作、編集、校正と様々な立場でこれまで15冊以上の書籍に関わってきましたが、そのすべてはオレンジバードのチームワークによって実現しています。本書も例外ではなく、オレンジバードの社内チーム及び外部の専門家との協働があって完成に至りました。本書で特筆すべきは、英文校正を担当いただいた言語学博士のエレナ・クラーク氏です。翻訳者や教育コンテンツクリエーターとして様々な場面でご一緒するクラーク博士からは、的確な校正はもちろん、内容に関しても有意義な助言を賜りました。また、版元であるベレ出版の編集チームの皆様にも御礼申し上げます。どのようにより有意義な書籍を作っていくかなど、企画段階から細部にわたるケアとサポートをいただきました。

本書において、説明の足りない（わかりにくい）記述、誤字脱字、その他不備があった場合、すべて著者に責任があります。至らぬ点としてお詫び申し上げます。お気づきの方は、ぜひ忌憚ないご指摘をお寄せください。

Introduction

本書の対象

Target

　書く・話すのアウトプットスキルは、学習の段階によって効き目のある学び方は大きく異なります。本書は、中級から中上級の学習者を想定して書いています。CEFRでいうとB2の真ん中くらいです。TOEIC L&Rではおおむね700点以上、IELTSバンド4.5以上、TOEFL iBTで言えば60 〜 65点程度の学習者をイメージしています。

　加えて、英語使用環境でいうと主にビジネスや学界で活躍する方を念頭に書いています。とりわけ、公務やビジネスで英語を使う、あるいは使いたいと考えている方、大学生、大学院生、企業・大学の研究者といった方には、すぐに取り入れていただける表現を集めました。

　また、ライティングのある検定試験の準備をしている方にも役立つ内容をたくさん盛り込んでいます。TOEFL-iBT、IELTS、英検準1級や1級の受験を控えている方には特におすすめです。ある程度英語力があって、今からはアウトプットスキルを伸ばしたいという方にぜひ使っていただきたいと願っています。

本書の狙い

　学習者にとって英語でアウトプットする際のフラストレーションの主因は、伝えたい内容と言葉として出てくる英語の落差です。年齢や社会的立場相応の内容を考えているのに、言葉に出してみたら何かとシンプルすぎて稚拙にすら聞こえる英語になってしまう現象です。これは、母語（日本語）と第二言語（英語）の習熟度の違いがそのまま具象化されるからです。

　アウトプットスキルが発揮される場面は多岐にわたります。ビジネスであれば顧客とのコミュニケーションや社内外の会議、学界ならゼミ

Purpose

やシンポジウム、学会発表、発表後の質疑応答、論文の準備や執筆などです。

　意見を言ったり質問に答えたりする場面では、よりロジカルにより明快に英語で話したいものです。ニュアンスを加味して理解できる、ニュアンスを付加して発言できる、そういった側面のレパートリーを増やしてスキルとして定着させることが本書の狙いです。

　アウトプットスキルを伸ばすための学習法は様々あり、一つに絞ることは困難です。たくさんインプット（読む・聞く）をしてボキャブラリーを増強させる、文法に磨きをかけて精度を高めるなど、多面的な練習を重ねてはじめて目に見える前進が図れます。表現方法の幅を意識的に広げていくことも、アウトプットスキル向上のための重要な項目のひとつです。

　本書は、ディスコースマーカー、指示語、ニュアンス付加の動詞など、アウトプットの「接着剤」となる表現に焦点を絞って、詳しく解説しています。

本書の使い方

　本書はシンプルな作りをしています。各Unitのテーマが決まっており、解説→例文→練習問題の順に進めていく構成です。「初めて知った」という内容は少ないと思います。過去に見聞きしたことのある表現について、ニュアンス、使い方、違いなどを本書で「深掘り」してください。解説を読んでから練習問題を解くことが重要です。練習問題の解答や日本語訳は巻末に掲載していますので、セルフチェックしてみましょう。また、リスニング問題は数回聞き、しっかり理解することを目指してください。テスト勉強ではないので、スピードより精度を重んじてゆっくり納得しながら読み進めることをおすすめします。

Method

目次

P. 077

文章や会話の流れを転換させるディスコースマーカーに着目します。お馴染みのbutを使いすぎる英語アウトプットから脱皮して、対照・否定表現を多く学び、練習することで、ニュアンスに富んだ洗練されたコミュニケーションを実現しましょう。

P. 092

英語では繰り返しを避けることがかなり重要視されます。Unit 10は、その反復回避の一つの方法である代名詞と参照フレーズを確認します。日本語はあまり代名詞を使わないため、参照表現としての使い方が身につくとより自然な英語が話せます。

P. 099

語義、語釈、定義を学び練習することで、機動力のあるアウトプットを実現します。続いて、類語、同義語、反対語の語彙を意識して増やし、より立体感のあるコミュニケーションを目指します。反復回避のみならず、積極的なボキャブラリー増強に役立つUnitです。

P. 107

間接話法を学び直すこのUnitでは、一般的な文法のルールをおさらいするに加え、間接話法の表現の幅を大きく広げていくことを目指します。伝え方のバリエーションが増えるので、日常的な会話にすぐに役立てることができます。

P. 124

第三者の発言に賞賛や批判など多彩なニュアンスを付加することができる動詞を取り上げます。文章でも会話でもよく使われる語彙ですので、しっかり学び練習することで、ワンランク上のコミュニケーションが可能となります。

P. 143

ビジネスや学界のコミュニケーションにおいて、図表などのビジュアルや何らかの数字について話すことがよくあります。数量や図表を言葉で表現しなおす手法の幅を広げることで、正確に伝わる、より円滑なコミュニケーションが実現します。

P. 169

最後のUnit 15では、1 〜 14までの各Unitの練習問題(Task)を解いて、本文で得た知識を定着させることができます。改めて各テーマの問題を解くことでより自信が持てるようになります。また、迷いがある場合は、そのUnitに戻って見直すきっかけにも使うことをおすすめします。

Index

付属音声のダウンロード方法

本書の音声は、スマートフォンやタブレット、またはパソコンで聞くことができます。音声は全て無料でお聞きいただけます。

スマートフォン・タブレットの場合

AI英語教材アプリabceed（株式会社Globee提供）ⓐ

Step 1 アプリストアで「abceed」をダウンロード。

Step 2 アプリを立ち上げ、本書の名前を検索して音声を使用。

英語アプリmikan

Step 1 アプリストアで「mikan」をダウンロード。

Step 2 アプリを立ち上げ、「教材一覧」の検索バーで本書の名前を検索。

Step 3 音声ボタン（♫）より、音声を再生。

パソコンの場合

「ベレ出版」ホームページ

Step 1 「ベレ出版」ホームページ内、『意見・主張をクリアに伝える技術 ディスコースマーカーで英語はこんなに伝わる』のページへ。 「音声ファイル」の「ダウンロード」ボタンをクリック。

https://www.beret.co.jp/

Step 2 8ケタのコードを入力して「ダウンロード」ボタンをクリック。

ダウンロードコード **v8p53LGk**

Step 3 ダウンロードされた圧縮ファイルを解凍して、 お使いの音声再生ソフトに取り込んで音声を使用。

※ダウンロードされた音声はMP3形式となります。
※ zip ファイルの解凍方法、MP3携帯プレイヤーへのファイル転送方法、各種ソフトの操作方法については小社での対応はできかねますこと、ご理解ください。
☞ 音声の権利・利用については、小社ホームページ内［よくある質問］にてご確認ください。

Unit 1

ディスカッション表現

英語の特徴の一つに、良い点と悪い点をできるだけ客観的に洗い出した上で意見を述べるということがあります。また、同じ単語の繰り返しを極力避け、多様な語彙を使って表現しようとするのも大きな特徴です。よく伝わる英語とは、これらの特徴をしっかり押さえたアウトプットそのものと言えます。このユニットでは、英語らしさを備えたアウトプットに欠かせない「ディスカッションのことば」を学んでいきます。

1 ディスカッションの表現

単語のディスカッション表現

もっとも一般的な表現ペアは、benefit － drawback と advantage － disadvantage です。単体でもペアとしてもよく出会います。

□ **benefit** /ˈbenɪfɪt/ 恩恵、利益、利点
□ **drawback** /ˈdrɔːbæk/ 不利な点、欠点、難点、短所
□ **advantage** /ədˈvæntɪdʒ/ 長所、利点、強み
□ **disadvantage** /ˌdɪsədˈvæntɪdʒ/ 不利な点、欠点、難点

○ Before we make a decision, let's discuss the advantages and the disadvantages.

判断をする前に短所と長所を議論しましょう。

○ We are well aware of the benefits of jogging, but we rarely look into the drawbacks.

私たちはジョギングの利点をよく知っていますが、欠点に目を向けることはまれです。

フレーズのディスカッション表現

良い点・悪い点は、フレーズで表現することもできます。

☐ positive aspect　プラス面
☐ negative aspect　マイナス面
☐ positive effect　プラス効果、良い結果
☐ negative effect　マイナス効果、悪い結果

○ 5G mobile networks will no doubt have a positive effect on e-commerce.
5G の移動体ネットワークが e コマースにプラス効果となるのは疑いない。

○ Noise pollution is a negative aspect of living near the highway.
騒音公害は高速道路の近くに住むことのマイナス面です。

フォーマルなディスカッション表現

賛否両論の表現には、フォーマルな場で使う少し「かたい英語」もあります。merit － demerit は代表例です。日本語だと「メリット」や「デメリット」という語彙は気軽に使ってしまいますが、英語だと書き言葉やオフィシャルな場で使うことが多いです。

☐ merit /ˈmerɪt/ 長所、利点
☐ demerit /diːˈmerɪt/ 短所、不利な点

また、merit は「実績」、demerit は北米では「罰点(学業・軍事記録に残る減点)」という意味でもよく使います。

○ We must take into account not only the merits but also the demerits if we are to contemplate an IPO.
株式公開を検討するのなら、メリットばかりではなく、デメリットも考慮すべきです。

インフォーマルなディスカッション表現

インフォーマルなビジネスディスカッションの場では、口語的な表現がよく用いられます。普段の会議や打ち合わせでは、advantage や disadvantage と肩を並べて登場します。なお、「賛否両論」といった意味合いで pros and cons という形（複数形）で使うことが多いです。

□ **pro** /prəʊ/ **メリット、利点**
□ **con** /kɑːn/ **デメリット、不利な点**
□ **plus** /plʌs/ **良さ、利点、強み**
□ **minus** /ˈmaɪnəs/ **欠点、弱点**
□ **upside** /ˈʌpsaɪd/ **（良くない状況の）良い側面**
□ **downside** /ˈdaʊnsaɪd/ **（良い状況の）良くない側面**

例

○ Speaking a foreign language can be a huge plus when looking for a new job.

外国語ができることは、新しい仕事を探す際大きな強みになり得る。

○ After discussing the pros and cons at length, we decided to decline the offer.

賛否両論をじっくり議論したすえ、我々は提案を断ることにしました。

○ The upside of the recent market downturn is that it presents an opportunity for savvy investors to buy stocks at a discount.

最近の市場低迷の救いは、賢明な投資家に株式を割安で購入する機会を提供していることです。

○ The downside of relying too heavily on technology is that it can lead to decreased face-to-face communication and social isolation.

テクノロジーに頼りすぎると、対面でのコミュニケーションが減り、社会的孤立を招くという弊害（＝良くない側面）があります。

2 ━━→ ディスカッション表現のニュアンス

形容詞を使ってディスカッション表現にニュアンスを加えることができます。

強める形容詞

はっきりとした、明確な、明白な

distinct /dɪˈstɪŋkt/   **clear** /dɪˈstɪŋkt/

相当な、重大な、大きな

major /ˈmeɪdʒər/   **significant** /sɪɡˈnɪfɪkənt/

substantial /səbˈstænʃl/

例

○ Peter is a certified accountant, which proved to be a significant advantage when he was applying for the CFO position.

ピーターは公認会計士で、この資格は財務担当役員のポストに応募した際に大きな利点となりました。

弱める、小さく見せる形容詞

極めて小さい、ほんのわずかな

minor /ˈmaɪnər/   **slight** /slaɪt/

例

○ Not having a flexible schedule might be a slight disadvantage for a freelance translator, but most employers focus more on the skillset.

スケジュールに柔軟性がないことはフリーランス翻訳者の場合は少し不利かもれませんが、多くの雇用主は主にスキルを見るのです。

重ねる形容詞（議論を展開する際に使えます）

更なる、追加の、加えての
　added /ˈædɪd/　　further /ˈfɜːrðər/

○ An added benefit of hiring Mr. Johnson would be his expertise on China.

中国事情に精通している点は、ジョンソンさんを雇うさらなる利点となるでしょう。

口語で使うニュアンスの形容詞

口語では、huge / small を使ってディスカッション表現にニュアンスを加えることがあります。

○ If we figure out what the shopping trends will be ahead of time, it would be a huge plus when we prep for the Christmas sale!

前もってショッピングの傾向がわかれば、クリスマスセールの準備の時にはめっちゃ役に立つでしょう!

───────────── Task 1 ─────────────

このユニットで学んだ以下のディスカッション表現を使って文を完成させましょう。同じ表現を 2 回以上使ってもかまいません。

benefit　drawback　advantage　disadvantage
positive aspect　negative aspect　pro　con　plus
minus　merit　demerit　upside　downside

1.

The main _____ of the new production line we installed is its maintenance cost. It's just too expensive.

2.

Many university students shared with us that homesickness is a major (1) _____ of studying abroad. The majority of students who have chosen to study outside of their country, however, do point out that the (2)_____s of studying abroad outweigh the (3)_____s.

3.

Good afternoon everyone! Thanks for joining me. I'd like us to discuss the (1) _____s and _____s of opening a new location in Singapore. At the moment, our London office is managing our business in Asia, but it has some serious (2)_____s in performing this task. One obvious (3)_____ is that it is physically too far from Asia. I believe that an office in Singapore may offer multiple (4)_____s and possibilities for us as a company. Please let me know what you think!

4.

We must carefully analyze the _____s of both proposals before drawing a conclusion. Figuring out potential problems is the best way to avoid risk.

5.

Solar energy may be a great sustainable solution, but we may be unaware of some of its _____s. Is the hardware safe for the environment? What about the running cost?

(Task 2)

質問を聞いて、適切な答えを選びましょう。

1. ◀) u0101

    A. Ms. Svenson submitted her CV last week.

    B. I honestly don't see any negative aspects to hiring her.

    C. She has a great potential as an artist.

2.  u0102

   A. I think it is because Poland offers many strategic advantages to foreign investors.

   B. Yes, the WDG Group is at an advantage because they are headquartered in Poland.

   C. The cold winter is a major drawback to growing plants in Poland.

3. 🔊 u0103

   A. The design of the car was amazing.

   B. There are a lot of advantages to buying a new car.

   C. The running cost is a major drawback, to be honest.

4. 🔊 u0104

   A. Yes, there are many benefits to being a CEO.

   B. I know what you mean. The disadvantages clearly outweighed the advantages.

   C. The new marketing plan was supported by everyone, no worries.

5. 🔊 u0105

   A. Yes, the time commitment such a project requires is a significant drawback for me.

   B. Yes, you are right, we must discuss the pros and cons before we agree.

   C. Let me ask you if you can see any drawbacks to participating in the project.

(Task 3)

トークを聞いて空所を埋めましょう。何回でも聞いてください。下線部には 2 語以上入る箇所もあります。 🔊 u0106

At the moment we are considering two possible locations for the new plant: Bangladesh and Taiwan. We need to discuss the _____ of both

options, and make a decision soon. While both Bangladesh and Taiwan offer _____ for us, I believe that Taiwan is the better option. Other members of the board believe that Bangladesh is better because it _____ of lower labor cost. In my opinion the _____ of choosing Taiwan would be the access to skilled labor that it offers. And skilled workers will give us a _____ that cannot be matched by Bangladesh. What do you think?

もう一度音声を聞いて以下の設問に答えましょう。

1. What is the main topic of the talk?
   A. Discussing where to move the current plant
   B. Discussing where to construct a new plant
   C. Discussing the economic situation in Bangladesh and Taiwan

2. Why do some people believe that Bangladesh is a better option?
   A. Because it offers access to cheaper labor.
   B. Because it has a bigger population.
   C. Because it offers a better climate.

3. What does the speaker believe about Taiwan?
   A. It has much cheaper labor than Bangladesh.
   B. It has more skilled workers than Bangladesh.
   C. It has a better economy than Bangladesh.

4. What has to happen soon?
   A. They have to visit Taiwan.
   B. They have to build the plant.
   C. They need to make a decision.

因果関係表現 ①

自らの意見をロジカルに述べる、他人と議論するなど、因果関係表現はさまざまな場面で役に立ちます。正しく使えると、ビジネスでもアカデミズムでもコミュニケーションが円滑に図れるようになります。because と because of は最もよく知られている 2 つの因果関係表現ですが、他にもたくさんあります。因果関係表現のレパートリーを増やして、表現力豊かな英語発話を目指しましょう。

因果関係表現においては、原因と結果という 2 つの主な要素があります。原因に重きを置くか結果に重きを置くかで使う構文などに違いが出てきますので、そのルールをしっかり覚えて正しいアウトプットを目指しましょう。「重きを置く」とは、何を主題として伝えようとしているかを示します。伝えている情報量は同じですが、先に結果を置くか原因を置くかで優先順位的なニュアンスが付加されます。その判断は、前後の文脈（例えば直前に聞かれた質問）、あるいは自らの言いたいこと次第で決めるのであって、ルールや正解不正解があるわけではありません。文脈や話の流れに沿った、唐突感を与えない語句を「先に」持ってくることによって、受け手により伝わりやすい自然な表現になります。

また、因果関係表現には、主に動詞（動詞句）と前置詞の 2 種類があります。使い分け方を覚えておくと便利です。

各種の因果関係表現に関して日本語訳を紹介していますが、文脈により他の訳し方が可能であるケースが多くあります。日本語訳に捕らわれることなく、なるべく英語ベースで理解していきましょう。

1 原因に重きを置く動詞の因果関係表現

原因表現を文頭に持ってくる

原因に重きを置く場合は、【原因＋因果関係動詞＋結果】というパターンを使います。動詞の三単現の s や、文意に合った時制を使っているかを確認しましょう。よく使われる因果関係表現の動詞には次のようなものがあります。

□ cause　引き起こす

□ lead to　〜につながる、〜を導く

□ result in　〜の結果をもたらす

□ produce　〜の結果を生む

□ can be seen as the cause for　〜の原因とみることができる

○ <u>Increased consumption of processed food</u>【原因】　<u>can be seen as the cause for</u>【因果関係表現動詞】　<u>the steady increase in obesity</u>【結果】.

加工食品の消費増加は、肥満が安定的に増え続けていることの原因とみることができる。

○ <u>The advent of AI-generated content</u>【原因】　<u>led to</u>【因果関係表現動詞】　<u>a decrease in the writing skills of the younger generation</u>【結果】.

AI 生成コンテンツの出現は、若い世代のライティングスキルの低下の要因となった。

○ <u>The lack of proper maintenance of the bus</u>【原因】　<u>can be seen as the main cause for</u>【因果関係表現動詞】　<u>the accident</u>【結果】.

事故が多発したのは、バスのメンテナンスが適切に行なわれていないことが主な原因だと考えられる。

seen を regarded に変えてもよく、cause for を driver behind に変えてもよいです。表現にバリエーションを持たせて相手を飽きさせない英語を話しましょう。

 2 ‧ **結果に重きを置く受動態の因果関係表現**

結果表現を文頭に持ってくる

結果に重きを置く場合は、【結果＋因果関係動詞の受動態＋原因】というパターンを使います。受動態を使うことが圧倒的に多いのですが、そうではない表現もあります。よく使われるものに以下があります。

☐ **can be attributed to** 〜によるものとみなされる、〜に帰する
☐ **is/was caused by** 〜によって引き起こされる・引き起こされた
☐ **can be explained by** 〜で説明できる

○ The cancellation of the flight【結果】 was caused by【過去受動態の動詞】 the severe weather conditions that made it unsafe for the aircraft to take off【原因】.
今回の欠航は、悪天候により航空機の離陸が危険な状態になったためです。

○ The success of the company can be explained by its focus on innovation and its ability to adapt quickly to changes in the market.
同社の成功は、イノベーションに重点を置き、市場の変化に素早く対応する能力によって説明することができる。

‧ ‧

原因・結果のどちらに重きを置いた文かを見極め、原因と結果を入れ替えて表現してみましょう。

【例】

The majority of traffic accidents are caused by reckless driving.

交通事故の大多数は無謀な運転によって引き起こされる。

元の文は、「結果」である交通事故に重きを置いた文なので、「原因」に重きを置く文に書き換えます。

🔁 Reckless driving leads to traffic accidents.

無謀な運転は交通事故を引き起こす。

これは一例で、他にも正解になり得る書き方がたくさんあります。

1.

Insufficient sleep results in decreased efficiency during the day.

🔁 _____

_____

2.

"Smartphone neck" is a pain in the neck caused by looking at a smartphone screen for a prolonged period of time.

🔁 _____

_____

3.

The rapid spread of internet connectivity can be seen as the main reason for the emergence of many online businesses.

🔁 _____

_____

4.

Eating too much sugar can cause diabetes.

🔁 _____

_____

5.

Reading widely leads to better vocabulary skills.

↻ _____

_____

6.

Singing for hours may cause pain in the throat.

↻ _____

_____

(Task 2)

質問を聞いて、適切な答えを選びましょう。

1. 🔊 u0201

    A. Her nose has a beautiful shape.

    B. Yes, a runny nose can destroy your sleep.

    C. One reason could be allergies.

2. 🔊 u0202

    A. Yes, he has great leadership skills, that's why.

    B. So was I. But lack of funding might have caused them to fail.

    C. Of course, that wouldn't be a problem, just shoot me an email.

3. 🔊 u0203

    A. It leads to "insulin resistance", which causes diabetes.

    B. That's why I recommend eating more vegetables.

    C. Yes, that's why it leads to diabetes, no doubt.

4. 🔊 u0204

    A. Walking briskly every day for about 20 minutes has helped me lose weight and tone up.

    B. Does it hurt when you walk? Maybe your legs are sore then.

    C. Typically, muscle soreness is caused by overworking the muscles. Didn't you go for a run yesterday?

5. 🔊 u0205

    A. I think the law says that there must be a fire extinguisher in every house.

    B. Yes, they said on the news it was caused by a lightning strike.

    C. Yes, I'd love to go to the mountain to get some fresh air.

Task 3

音声を聞いて空所を埋めましょう。何回でも聞いてください。下線部には 2 語以上入る箇所もあります。 🔊 u0206

Excessive consumption of sugar _____ many harmful effects on human health. The sugar intake of people in developed countries has been increasing since the second half of the 20th century. This is _____ for the so-called obesity epidemic. The spread of obesity, in turn, _____ a number of diseases and conditions. In addition to being the _____ for type 2 diabetes, obesity is regarded _____ behind the surge in cancer, heart disease, and other serious conditions.

もう一度音声を聞いて以下の設問に答えましょう。

1. What is the main topic of the talk?
   A. How sugar was brought into Europe from the Caribbean.
   B. The importance of sugar as a major commodity, central to many economies.
   C. How sugar is harmful to the human body.

2. Which of the following is true about sugar intake?
   A. It has been on the rise since the second half of the 20th century.
   B. It was much higher in the Middle Ages.
   C. It has declined over the course of the last four decades.

3. Obesity is mentioned as the main cause of which disease?
   A. heart disease
   B. type 2 diabetes
   C. cancer

4. What is the author's opinion of sugar?
   A. The author believes sugar is a driver of civilization.
   B. Sugar is a ubiquitous chemical compound, according to the author.
   C. The author sees sugar as a major health hazard.

因果関係表現 ②

前の Unit では因果関係表現のうち、動詞や動詞句を中心にみてきました。この Unit では、接続詞を使った因果関係表現をおさらいします。動詞と同じく、「原因に重きを置く」タイプの構文と「結果に重きを置く」タイプの構文に分かれます。動詞表現と併せてマスターしておきましょう。文頭に結果を持ってくるか原因を持ってくるかで変わるのは、情報量ではなく、発言者が何に重きを置くかだと改めて認識しましょう。例えば、「友達に手伝ってもらったお陰でより良い成績を獲得できた」と言いたいとき、Thanks to your help, I was able to get better grades. と I was able to get better grades, thanks to your help. を比べてみると、伝えている情報はまったく同じですが、Thanks to your help を文頭に持ってきている方が相手に感謝を伝えたい場合はより適切な表現です。こうして、重きを置きたい要素を文頭にもってきて、優先順位を高くすることでニュアンスを付加することができます。

1 接続詞の因果関係表現

原因に重きを置く

原因に重きを置く場合、【因果関係接続詞＋原因＋結果】というパターンを使います。よく使われる接続詞には次のようなものがあります。

~の結果、~ゆえに、~の影響で

owing to　　due to　　because of

as a result of　　as a consequence of　　thanks to

thanks to は通常ポジティブな事柄に使います。owing to や due to は中立的なので、良いことにも悪いことにも使えます。

○ Due to【因果関係接続詞】 the influx of tourists to Kyoto【原因】, many local residents are complaining about noise pollution【結果】.
京都への観光客の流入により、多くの地元住民が騒音被害を訴えています。

○ Thanks to【因果関係接続詞】 your guidance【原因】, I was able to finish the project in time【結果】.
ご指導いただいたおかげで、時間内に完成させることができました。

○ As a result of【因果関係接続詞】 the advertising campaign【原因】, the company was able to acquire a number of new clients【結果】.
広告キャンペーンの結果、その会社は多くの新規顧客を獲得することができました。

結果に重きを置く

結果に重きを置く場合、【結果＋因果関係接続詞＋原因】というパターンを使います。

○ We believe that the failure in the conveyor belt【結果】 was because of【因果関係接続詞】 metal fatigue【原因】.
今回のベルトコンベアの故障は、金属疲労によるものだと考えています。

○ The athlete's improved performance【結果】 is definitely due to【因果関係接続詞】 the novel training methods of her new coach【原因】.
この選手のパフォーマンスが向上したのは、新しいコーチの斬新なトレーニング方法のおかげであることは間違いありません。

○ The floods and droughts all across Europe【結果】 are a consequence of【因果関係接続詞】 climate change【原因】, according to scientists.

科学者によると、ヨーロッパ全土で発生している洪水や干ばつは、気候変動の影響によるものだそうです。

② 一般化と具体化 – 因果関係表現の違い

一般的な話をするか、具体的な話をするかによって、因果関係表現の使い方が異なります。主な傾向として、接続詞（句）はより具体的な場面の表現に使い、動詞は一般的な状況（そもそも論）を指す傾向にあります。あくまでも傾向であって厳密なルールではありませんが、話す・書く際に意識しておくとよりわかりやすい英語になります。

一般化表現

いつもあることや普遍的な事実、当然と言えるようなことなどが中心です。単純現在や単純過去といった時制と組み合わせるとより自然に聞こえます。

○ Regular exercise leads to better health.

定期的な運動は、より良い健康状態につながります。

○ Sitting all the time leads to lower back pain.

座ってばかりいると腰が痛くなります。

さらに一般化された表現

might result in など、法助動詞を活用してさらに確度を下げて、「可能性」に近い表現に仕立てていくこともできます。

○ Losing weight tends to result in improved health.

（体重の）減量は、健康状態の改善につながる傾向にある。

具体化表現

「そもそも論」ではなく、具体的でよりリアリティのある話をする時に接続詞の表現を使います。

○ The high levels of air pollution in the city are a direct consequence of the increase in traffic.

市内の空気汚染が高レベルであるのは、交通量の増加が直接の原因です。

○ The company's profits have decreased as a result of the recent economic downturn and worsened consumer spending.

会社の利益は、最近の景気低迷と消費支出悪化の結果、減少しました。

○ I'm really happy because I reconnected with an old friend.

昔の友達と再会できたので、本当に嬉しいです。

その他の典型的な因果関係表現

☐ consequently　それ故に、その結果
☐ because　なぜなら
☐ if A occurs, then B　Aが発生するとB
☐ since　なので
☐ for this reason　そのため
☐ for　なので

○ Since the train was delayed, I arrived late for my appointment.

電車が遅れたため、予約に遅れてしまいました。

○ If you don't water the plants regularly, they will wither and die.

定期的に水をやらないと、植物はしおれて枯れてしまいます。

○She spent all her savings on unnecessary things. As a result (= consequently), she couldn't afford to pay her rent.

彼女は無駄な物に全ての貯金を使ってしまいました。その結果、彼女は家賃を払う余裕がありませんでした。

• ────── Task 1 ────── •

正しいペアを見つけて、文を作りましょう。ペアごとに結果に重きを置く文と原因に重きを置く文を作ってみましょう(計2つ)。動詞、名詞、時制の形を適宜調整しましょう。

【接続詞】

owing to　　due to　　because of　　as a result of

as a consequence of　　thanks to

【動詞】

cause　　lead to　　result in　　produce

can be seen as the cause for

the heavy rainfall	she was promoted to manager
negative effects on mental health	a decline in bee populations
the company's decision to cut costs	the excessive use of technology has been shown
she felt groggy and unproductive throughout the day	the ubiquitous availability of interactive digital maps
the widespread use of pesticides	severe flooding in the city
her dedication and hard work	the layoff of several employees
GPS-enabled devices	the teacher's strict grading policies
the students' high levels of stress	the lack of sleep

【例】

The ubiquitous availability of interactive digital maps is a consequence of GPS-enabled devices.

↻ GPS-enabled devices have led to the ubiquitous availability of interactive digital maps.

The ubiquitous availability of interactive digital maps is a direct result of GPS-enabled devices.

↻ GPS-enable devices can be seen as the cause for the ubiquitous availability of interactive digital maps.

1.1.

_____

_____

1.2.

↻ _____

_____

2.1.

_____

_____

2.2.

↻ _____

_____

3.1.

_____

_____

3.2.

↻ _____

_____

4.1.

_____

_____

4.2.

↻ _____

_____

5.1.

_____

_____

5.2.

↻ _____

_____

6.1.

_____

_____

6.2.

↻ _____

_____

7.1.

_____

_____

7.2.

↻ _____

_____

• (Task 2) •

次の文を読んで、原因に重きを置いたものなら、結果に重きを置くものに書き換え、結果に重きを置くものなら原因に重きを置くものに書き換えましょう。

【例】

Due to climate change, the sea level is rising.

↻ The rising in sea level is caused by climate change.

The overuse of smartphones can be seen as the cause of an increase in anxiety and depression among young adults.

↻ The increase in anxiety and depression among young adults can be attributed to the overuse of smartphones.

1.

Thanks to advancements in AI technology, self-driving cars are now able to navigate roads safely and efficiently.

↻ Self-driving cars _____

_____

2.

The high demand for electric vehicles has led to an increase in the production of lithium-ion batteries.

↻ The increase in the production of lithium-ion batteries _____

_____

3.

The development of advanced sensors has produced more accurate weather forecasting models.

↻ More accurate weather forecasting models _____

_____

4.

The recent surge in cryptocurrency prices can be attributed to the increasing popularity of blockchain technology.

↻ The increasing popularity of blockchain technology_____

_____

5.

The decrease in the use of fossil fuels has been brought about by the rising concern for climate change.

↻ The rising concern for climate change _____

_____

比較表現

学術的な説明やビジネスコミュニケーションにおいて伝えたい内容を具体化させたいとき、比較表現を有効活用できると説得力が高まります。形容詞の形としての比較級と最上級が代表的な比較表現ですが、この Unit では、それらに加えて、比較にニュアンスを添え、より高い精度で伝わる比較表現を探っていきます。また、形容詞の形以外の比較表現など、アウトプットのレパートリーにいくつかの便利なツールを加え、表現の幅を広げましょう。

1 ── 比較級と最上級の形

形容詞の形を改めておさらい

単音節の形容詞および y で終わる 2 音節の形容詞(y が i に変わる)〜 er(比較級)と〜 est(最上級)を使い、他の形容詞は more と most を使います。

> big – bigger – biggest   fast – faster – fastest   tall – taller - tallest
> happy – happier – happiest   funny – funnier – funniest
> positive – more positive – most positive
> complex – more complex – most complex

最上級と定冠詞 the ─ the を付けるとき・付けないとき

最上級は多く the を伴いますが、必ずではありません。通常は the を付けますが、所有格があるときは the を付けません。the を付けるかどうかを正しくかつ瞬時に判断できると日常会話やビジネスコミュニケーションがぐんとラクになります。

○ Tom Clancy is **the most** prolific author I have ever read.

　（Tom Clancy is **most prolific** は誤りです）

○ Kate is **the fastest** runner on the team.

　（Kate is **fastest** は誤りです）

○ Tim is my **best** employee.

　（Tim is my the best employee. は誤りです。所有格なので the を付けません）

○ This is Murakami's **most praised** novel so far.

　（This is Murakami's **the most praised** novel so far. は誤りです。所有格なので the を付
　けません）

叙述的な位置において、同じ人や物を別の場面と比べる時は、原則的に、the は付き
ません。the を付けると厳密には誤りであっても、口語においては the を付ける人もいます。

○ The baby is **nicest** when she is well-fed.

　（is **the nicest** …は誤りです。これは一人の人物の気分や挙動を別の場面と比べています）

○ Mary is **the nicest** of my classmates.

　（is **nicest** of は誤りです。 一人の人を別の数人と比較しています）

② 比較級のニュアンスを作る他の表現

副詞を使って精度を高める

比較級の形容詞にニュアンス（強弱など）を加えるには、副詞や副詞句を使います。

○ 例

○ A is bigger than B. → AとBの違いが 2% か 80% か分からない。

○ A is **significantly** bigger than B. → significantly 相当に、かなり

○ A is **slightly** bigger than B. → slightly 少し

【意味を強める副詞の例】

significantly　substantially　much

by an order of magnitude　considerably

【意味を弱める副詞の例】

slightly　marginally　infinitesimally

【中立的な副詞（句）】

by XX%

形容詞を使わずに比較する

比較級と最上級を使わない比較の表現には、"as … as" および "the same as" があります。同等またはほぼ同等のものの比較に使います。

○ 例

○ A is **as durable as** B.　AはBと同じくらい耐久性がある。

○ A is **the same acidity as** B.　AはBと同じ酸度です。

○ A is **half as big as** B. (= A is 50% of the size of B)　AはBの半分の大きさです。

3 ── 比較表現を使った文の立て方

比較級を使った表現の柔軟性

比較の文を構成するアプローチはたくさん存在します。例えば、「私は妹より背が低い」と言いたいとしましょう。

○ My sister is taller than me. I am shorter than my sister.
○ When compared to me, my sister is taller.
○ My sister is the taller of the two of us.

いずれも正しい表現です。

4 ・ 抽象的概念の比較

文脈で選ぶ比較級のバリエーション

high と low は抽象的な概念を比較するのに使います。また、more と less はよく than と組み合わせて使います。

□ higher / lower　順位やレベルの比較

higher priority　より高い優先度　　lower risk　低いリスク
higher density　より高い密度

□ higher / lower　値などに加え、抽象的な価値や度合の比較

higher cost　高いコスト　　lower benefit　低い利益

□ better / worse　質や好ましさの比較

better idea　より良いアイデア　　worse outcome　より悪い結果

☐ stronger / weaker　度合、強度の比較

stronger argument　より強力な論旨　　weaker case　より弱いケース

weaker drink　よりアルコール度数の低い飲み物

☐ more / less　通常の分量比較に加え、抽象的なものの度合の比較

more important　より重要　　less significant　それほど重要ではない

☐ broader / narrower　範囲の比較

broader perspective　より広い視点　　narrower focus　より絞られた焦点

☐ deeper / shallower　深みや度合の比較

deeper understanding　より深い理解

shallower analysis　より浅い（表面的な）分析

☐ greater / smaller
視覚的に確認できるサイズに加え、抽象的な重要性や度合の比較

greater impact　より大きな影響　　smaller effect　より小さな効果

• (Task 1) •

空欄に入る正しい選択肢を選びましょう。

1.

After I reviewed the results, I wasn't _____ before.

    A. same confident as

    B. as confident as

    C. the most confident

2.

Learning how to communicate effectively is much _____ than having a vast knowledge of information.

    A. importanter

    B. more important

    C. as important as

3.

Although the new smartphone has a _____ screen than its predecessor, their overall dimensions are still comparable.

    A. significantly bigger

    B. substantially smaller

    C. slightly bigger

4.

Learning a new language as an adult is much _____ than learning it as a child.

    A. more difficult

    B. substantially difficult

    C. less difficult

5.

Running a marathon was not _____ I imagined it would be, thanks to my rigorous training regimen.

    A. less hard than

    B. as hard as

    C. substantially less hard than

6.

The group exposed to the highest concentration of the chemical in the experiment showed _____ adverse effects as the group exposed to the lowest concentration.

    A. twice as much

    B. not enough

    C. significantly more bigger

Task 2

下記の表を使って、各国の大卒人口を比較する文を完成させましょう。下線部には 2 語以上入る箇所があります。

Country	University graduates holding a 4-year degree
Australia	39%
Brazil	16%
Greece	39%
Indonesia	11%
Spain	28%
Poland	43%
Saudi Arabia	26%
Slovenia	34%

（出典：*List of countries and dependencies by population*）

1. Poland has _____ percentage of university graduates among these countries.
2. Greece has _____ percentage of university graduates as Australia.
3. Indonesia has _____ percentage of university graduates, compared to Slovenia.
4. The percentage of university graduates in Brazil is _____ than Indonesia.
5. Saudi Arabia's percentage is _____ compared to Poland.
6. The percentage of Spain is _____ than that of Slovenia.
7. Australia and Greece both have a _____ percentage of university graduates than Brazil.
8. Saudi Arabia's percentage is _____ double compared to Indonesia.

--•(Task 3)•--

会話を聞いて、適切な答えを選びましょう。

1. ◀)) u0401
   A. The dress costs the same amount.
   B. The dress costs less.
   C. The dress is twice as expensive.

2. ◀)) u0402
   A. The game will be a blowout victory for their team.
   B. The game will be slightly closer than the previous one.
   C. The game will be a close victory for their team.

3. ◀)) u0403
   A. The new laptop is significantly more powerful than the old one.
   B. The new laptop is slightly more powerful than the old one.
   C. The new laptop is the same as the old one.

4. 🔊 u0404

    A. The traffic is less congested than in Chattanooga.

    B. The traffic is the same as in Chattanooga.

    C. The traffic is significantly worse in LA.

5. 🔊 u0405

    A. Austin and Phoenix are in very close proximity.

    B. Austin is as big as Phoenix in terms of population.

    C. Phoenix and Austin are equally popular.

if/when/wish 現実と架空

次の会話を読んで、何が違うか比べてみましょう。

A：Does John know about the party tomorrow?

B：I don't think he does. I'll let him know if I see him at the office today!

C：John didn't come to the party yesterday. I have the feeling that he didn't know there was one.

D：Yeah, I imagine he would have come, if he had known – John loves parties.

A と B は現在や未来の話をしており、「現実」の話です。B が John に会う保証はありませんが、「会ったら伝えておくよ」と現実的にあり得ることとして言っています。一方、C と D の会話は過去の話題を扱っています。D の発言は過去において状況が違っていたらというものなので、「架空」です。

条件法には 2 つの大きな基軸が存在します。一つ目は、話が現在と未来なのか、それとも過去なのか、二つ目は、状況が現実か架空かです。

1 ─ 現在・未来における条件表現

現実の発言 if/when

○ My phone is really old. If I buy a new one, I'll be able to take much better pictures.

私の携帯は本当に古いんです。新しいのを買ったら、もっといい写真が撮れるようになるんだろうな。

- if は when より確度が低く、when を使うとそういった予定があるというニュアンスが伝わります。when は架空の状況を表す文では使いません。
- if 節で現在形を使います。その他は伝えたい意味によって現在形と未来形を使い分けます。以下の例文も見てみましょう。

○ Please let me know if/when Ann comes.　Ann が来たら教えてください。
発言者は、Ann が来ることを知っており、来たタイミングで知らせてほしいと言っています。

○ Please let me know if Ann will come.　Ann が来るかどうか教えてください。
発言者は、Ann が来るかどうかが分からないので、それについて教えてほしいと言っています。

架空の状況

○ If I had a million dollars, I would buy a beach house.
100 万ドルあったら、ビーチハウスを買いたいですね。

100 万ドルを持っているわけではないのですが、100 万ドルを持っていたらと想像するとビーチハウスを買うだろうと言っています。

「架空」を表す言い方を使う意味は、客観的に非現実的というより、発言者の伝えたい意図を指します。上記例文中の If I had a million dollars は、発言者は 100 万ドルを自分が持っているわけがないと思っていることを伝えており、そもそも人間は 100 万ドルを持ち得ないという意味ではありません。

現在と未来の話で、かつ架空の状況に関する発言では、If 節で単純過去を使います。be 動詞の一人称は、were と was が両方とも使われています。were の方が文法的に正しいとされていますが、日常コミュニケーションにおいてはほとんど同等の扱いです。条件法で使われる単純過去は、あくまでも文法的な形であって、過去の出来事を指さず、現在と未来の出来事しか表現していません。

○ If I were you, I would not apply for this position.

　私があなたなら、この仕事には応募しなかったでしょう。

○ If you paid more attention during class, you could get better grades.

　授業中にもっと注意を払っていれば、より良い成績が取れるかもしれません。

架空の状況の場合は would を使います。could と might も使えます。その 3 つの中で、would の確度が一番高く、次に could、そして might が使われます。

wish, if only

条件法で架空の状況を表す場合、【wish+ 単純過去】もよく使われます。if だとニュートラルな発言として伝わりますが、wish だと少し感情的です。強い希望、後悔などが効率よく伝わります。比べてみましょう。

○ If I were fluent in French, I would not read Descartes translated into English.

　フランス語に堪能だったら、英語に翻訳されたデカルトは読まないでしょうね。

○ I wish I were better at French!

　フランス語がもっと上手だったらなあ!

いずれも、フランス語の語学力が足りないといったことを伝えていますが、I wish の方が個人的な感情がこもります。

○ I wish I didn't have to pay my bills, but sadly I do.

　クレジットカードの請求書を支払う必要がなかったらよかったのですが、残念ながら支払わなければなりません。

if only も後悔や強い希望の表現としてよく使われます。実質的に wish と同じく、より感情的なニュアンスです。if only を使う場合、通常は would 節を用いません。

○ If only I had some more money. もう少しお金あればいいのにな。

過去の条件法

過去は過ぎ去った時間を指す時間概念ですので、条件法では「現実」の文が立てられません。私たちは過去を完全に把握しているという前提で使うので、過去の出来事に関する条件法の文は「架空」となります。

○ I would have called you, if had known about the meeting.
会議のことを知っていたら、連絡してあげたのに。

発言者は、相手に連絡をしなかったのは、自分も会議のことを把握していなかったからだ、という意味が伝わります。
if/wish の節では過去完了 (had been, had known) を使い、would 節では、現在完了 (would have been, would have done) を使います。

○ Do you wish you had chosen another job?
他の仕事にしたら良かったのに、と思うことはありますか?

○ I wish I had studied more math at school.
学校でもっと数学をやれば良かったのに。

条件法における時制をもう一度振り返ってみましょう。would (do, be) は現在を指し、would have (been, done) は過去を指します。

例

○ I would definitely go to the party, if I were in town tomorrow.

明日街にいればパーティーに絶対参加するのに。

○ I would definitely have joined the party, if I had been in town yesterday.

昨日街にいればパーティーに絶対参加したのに。

───────────────── (Task 1) •──────

カッコ内の動詞を正しい形にしましょう。

【例】

I have no idea how to reach him. If I __knew (know)__ his phone number,
I __would call (call)__ him right away.

1.

During the meeting yesterday I was supposed to present my marketing
ideas about the new product. I had nothing to say, and I was so embarrassed.
I wish I __(prepare)__ for the meeting.

2.

What __(you say)__ if you could talk to the President of the United States?

3.

I would buy this house if it __(be)__ less expensive.

4.

If I had had more time, I __(study)__ more for my exams.

5.

If she __(be)__ taller, she could reach the top shelf.

6.

If it __(rain)__ tomorrow, I won't go to the park.

7.

If he __(have)__ a car, he could drive us to the beach.

8.

If we __(leave)__ early, we could have beaten the traffic.

9.

If they __(meet)__ earlier, they could have gone to the concert together.

10.

If I __(win)__ the lottery, I would travel the world.

11.

If you __(listen)__ to me, you wouldn't have made that mistake.

12.

If the weather __(be)__ better, we could have a picnic.

13.

If she __(speak)__ Spanish, she could communicate better with her grandmother.

14.

If she __(like)__ spicy food, I would recommend this dish to her.

15.

If he __(know)__ the answer, he would have raised his hand.

16.

If we __(arrive)__ earlier, we could have watched the whole movie.

17.

If they __(finish)__ their work, they can go home early.

18.

If I __(have)__ a magic wand, I would make everyone happy.

19.

If the sky __(be)__ clear tonight, we will see the solar eclipse.

(Task 2)

下記の空所に when もしくは if のどちらか適切な方を入れましょう。

1.

I'll go to the store _____ I have time.

2.

_____ it rains, we'll stay inside.

3.

I'll call you _____ I arrive at the airport.

4.

_____ you need help, just ask.

5.

_____ I see her, I'll give her the message.

6.

We'll have a party _____ we finish the project.

7.

I would help you _____ I could.

8.

I'll buy a new car _____ I have enough money.

9.

_____ I finish my homework by 8, I'll watch a movie.

10.

_____ you finish your dinner, we can go for a walk.

11.

_____ you're ready, let's start the presentation.

12.

_____ she arrives earlier than 5 pm, please give me a call.

Unit 6

ifを使わない条件表現

条件を表現するには、if や wish を使わない方法もあります。文法の違いに注目しながら眺めていきましょう。

1 ── in case, as long as, provided, providing を使った表現

前提条件を示す表現

in case, as long as, provided, providing を使って条件を表現することができます。いずれも現実的な状況を指すので、「架空の状況」の際に使う文法は登場しません。主節には will や can を使い、【would (should) have+ 過去分詞】といった架空の状況を示す動詞は使いません。

in case は比較的カジュアルな場面から硬い場面まで使えますが、as long as, provided, providing ほど絶対的な条件を表しておらず、「事前の対策や備え」を表現することが多いです。

一方、as long as, provided, providing は、前提条件を置くために使います。また、provided と providing は意味と使い方が同じですが、provided の方がよく使われます。例を見てみましょう。

○ I'll lend you my car **provided that** you promise to return it on time.

時間通りに返すと約束してくれれば、私の車を貸しても良いです。

○ **Providing that** the weather is good, we'll have a picnic in the park.

天気が良ければ、公園でピクニックをしましょう。

○ You can use my bike **provided that** you wear a helmet.

ヘルメットをかぶれば、私の自転車を使ってもいいよ。

○ You'll receive a bonus **provided that** you meet your sales targets.

売上目標を達成したら、ボーナスを支給します。

○ I will continue to work at this company **as long as** I am happy with my job and salary.

仕事と給料に満足している限り、この会社で働き続けるつもりです。

provided (providing) that, if, only if, as long as は使えますが、in case は使えません。

○ **In case** it rains, I will bring an umbrella with me.

雨が降る場合に備えて、傘を持っていきます。

○ **In case** you need my help, don't hesitate to call me.

何か困ったことがあったら、遠慮なく電話してください。

in case は使えますが、provided (providing) that, if, as long as は使えません。

---

2 • 倒置構文

倒置構文を利用した条件法

倒置構文を使った表現は、「硬い」「文語的だ」とよく言われます。硬いと見るかどうかはある意味主観ですが、現実的によく使われるので、自分でも使えるようにしっかり理解しておきましょう。

○ **If I had known about the accident**, I would have never asked him such silly questions.

↻ **Had I known about the accident**, I would have never asked him such silly questions.

事故のことを知っていれば、こんなバカな質問はしなかっただろう。

if 節から if をなくして、倒置構文(疑問文で使う語順)にすることで、条件法を表現します。上の文は下の文とまったく同じ意味です。こういった倒置構文の条件法は、過去における架空の状況を示す場合のみ使います。現在や未来を指す表現では使いません。would 節は影響を受けず、if を使う文と変わりありません。

○ If I had studied harder, I would have passed the exam with flying colors.

↻ Had I studied harder, I would have passed the exam with flying colors.

もっと勉強していれば、見事に合格していたはずです。

映画『ミッション：インポッシブル』では、スパイにミッションを伝えるために「Your mission, should you choose to accept it,…. 」という言葉を使っています。この should は、通常の時の should と違って、「べき」や「〜なければならない」という意味がありません。if を使わない条件法です。つまり、「Your mission, if you choose to accept it, …. 」と同じく、「受け入れるのなら、あなたのミッションは…」という意味です。もう少し実生活に近い例を読んでみましょう。

○ Should you have any questions, please contact our sales team.
　ご不明な点は、弊社営業担当までお問い合わせください。

こちらも「倒置構文」を使って、you should という肯定文の語順ではなく、should you という疑問文と同じ語順になっています。ただここでは、should は if の意味を担って肯定文を成しています。普通は、should を使った条件表現を使って聞き手に対する「〜したらいいですよ」や「〜してください」のような呼び掛けをします。『ミッション：インポッシブル』のように、他の条件表現の代わりに使うことはあり得ますが、さほど多くありません。

should は多くの場合、in case や if に言い換えることができます。should を使った条件法はフォーマルな印象を与えるので、日常コミュニケーションではあまり使いません。

○ Should you need any assistance, do not hesitate to ask.
　何か困ったことがあったら、遠慮なく声をかけてください。

○ Should any emergency arise, evacuate immediately.
　緊急事態が発生した場合は、すぐに避難してください。

○ Should you come across any difficulty, reach out to a friend for help.
　困ったことがあったら、友だちに助けを求めてください。

その他の条件表現

時には、if 節や倒置構文を使わず条件を表現することがあります。

○ Thanks for letting me know. Without this information, I wouldn't have understood what he meant.
　教えてくれてありがとう。その情報がなければ、彼の言っていることが理解できなかったと思います。

If I hadn't had this information, I wouldn't have understood what he meant. とまったく同じ意味ですが、if を使わなくても当然理解されるという前提の文です。

次は、otherwise(そうでなければ、さもなくば)を使っての条件表現です。otherwise の場合も、would 節の動詞は影響を受けず、if を使う文と同じ形を取ります。

○ I'm glad I brought my umbrella; otherwise, I would have gotten wet in the rain.

傘を持ってきて良かった。そうしなければ、雨に濡れるところだった。

○ I made a reservation in advance; otherwise, I wouldn't have gotten a table at the restaurant.

事前に予約を入れておいた。そうでなければ、そのレストランでテーブルを確保できなかっただろう。

○ I had to leave home early; otherwise, I would have missed my flight.

早く家を出なければならなかった。そうでなければ、飛行機に乗り遅れるところだった。

Task 1

下記の文を読み、in case、as long as、provided、providing の使い方が間違っているものを見つけましょう。文が合っていれば Correct に○をし、間違っていれば Incorrect に○をしましょう。

Sentence	Correct	Incorrect
1. I always carry a spare tire in my trunk, **provided** I get a flat on the road.		○
2. **In case of** a power outage, the backup generator will automatically kick in to keep the lights on.		
3. I will email you a copy of the report **as long as** you need it for your records.		
4. You can use the company car **provided that** you follow the rules and regulations.		

5. **Providing** you need to contact me during the trip, my cell phone will have international roaming enabled.		
6. I will lend you the money **in case** you pay me back within a month.		
7. The discount is valid **provided that** you present this coupon at the time of purchase.		
8. **As long as** there are no technical difficulties, the online class should run smoothly.		
9. **In case** you study hard, you will do well on the exam.		
10. I will continue to support you **as long as** you make a genuine effort to change.		

• (Task 2) •

次の発言を聞いて、正しい言い換えを選びましょう。

【例】 ◀)) I saved up for the trip, and that is why I was able to go.

  A. Should I have saved for that trip, I would have been able to go.

  ✓ B. I saved up for that trip. Otherwise, I wouldn't have been able to go.

  C. Had I saved up for that trip, I wouldn't have been able to go.

---

1. ◀)) u0601

  A. If he hadn't told me the truth, I would still have been in the dark.

  B. Had he told me truth, I would still be in the dark.

  C. If I knew the truth, I would still be in the dark.

2. ◀)) u0602

  A. Even if I was informed, I would have made the same mistake.

  B. If I had made such a costly mistake earlier, I would have known better.

  C. Had I been more informed, I wouldn't have made such a costly mistake.

3. 🔊 u0603

    A. Had he taken that job, he wouldn't have met his future wife.

    B. If he hadn't taken that job, he wouldn't have met his future wife.

    C. Should he have taken that job, he wouldn't have met his future wife.

4. 🔊 u0604

    A. Should you decide to change your plans, let us know as soon as possible.

    B. If you tell us about your plans, we will let you know right away.

    C. If your plans haven't changed, you should let us know.

5. 🔊 u0605

    A. If you don't have time, we do not want your feedback on our proposal.

    B. Should you have time, we would appreciate your feedback on our proposal.

    C. It would have been nice if you had provided feedback on our proposal.

6. 🔊 u0606

    A. Had we gone to the museum, we wouldn't have discovered that new artist.

    B. If we had discovered that new artist, we wouldn't have gone to the museum.

    C. It's great that we went to that museum. Otherwise, we wouldn't have discovered that new artist.

if を使わない条件表現

質問を使った表現

質問は疑問文を使い、通常は会話において相手の答えを誘発するために使います。しかし疑問文の応用範囲は実はもっと広く、いろいろな役割を果たすことができます。日本語でも質問をまったく同じように使うので、英語特有の現象ではありません。ここで紹介する3つの役割をマスターすると、質問を使ってより豊かな表現ができます。

サジェスチョンやお誘い
(例)Why don't we…? What about …? How about …?

意見を質問で表すナラティブ誘導型質問(修辞疑問文)
(例)Why would I?

1 ── サジェスチョンやお誘い

質問を意図しない疑問文(提案・お誘い)

日本語でも、「ご飯食べにいきませんか?」といった疑問文は、形式的に YES/NO の質問ですが、本質的な役割は「お誘い」です。つまり、「ご飯食べにいこうよ!」と同じ意味です。英語では、why, how about, what about などを使ってこういったサジェスチョン(提言、提案)とお誘いを表現します。

○ Why don't we plan a picnic this weekend?
今週末はピクニックを企画しませんか?

○ How about taking a cooking class together?

一緒に料理教室に通うのはどうだろう?

○ What about trying that new restaurant downtown?

街中の新しいレストランを試してみるのはどうだろう?

○ Why don't we go on a hike next Sunday?

次の日曜日はハイキングに行かない?

 2 ━━ ナラティブ誘導型質問 (修辞疑問文)

自問自答のための疑問文

英語では、rhetorical question と言います。これは、語り手や書き手が質問を訊いて、自分で答えていくというもので、「ナラティブ誘導型質問」です。質問を訊いていくことにより、聞き手にこれから触れていく話題を知らせたりして、話が進む方向性を示しています。いくつか例を読んでみましょう

○ **Why do we go through life searching for answers? Is it because we want to know the truth, or is it because we fear the unknown? We are constantly searching for answers, but do we ever stop to think if we are ready for the truth?** Perhaps sometimes it's better to leave some questions unanswered.

私たちはなぜ、答えを探しながら生きているのでしょうか。真実を知りたいからでしょうか、それとも未知なるものを恐れているからでしょうか。私たちは常に答えを探し求めていますが、自分が真実を知る準備ができているかどうか、立ち止まって考えたことはあるでしょうか。ときには、答えのないままにしておいたほうがいいこともあるのです。

○ I want to buy a new car. It needs to be much bigger than the one I have now. **But why do I need a new car now?** Well, it's because I've taken up a new hobby.

車を買い換えたい。今持っている車よりずっと大きいのが欲しい。**でも、なぜ今、新しい車が必要なのか。**それは、新しい趣味を始めたからだ。

○ **Why do we accumulate possessions? Is it because we believe they bring us happiness and security?** We all have things we hold dear, but do we ever consider the weight they carry on our lives? Perhaps it's time to reevaluate what truly brings us joy and contentment.

人はなぜ財産を蓄えるのでしょうか。それが幸せや安心をもたらすと信じているからでしょうか。私たちは皆、大切なものを持っています。しかし、それらが私たちの人生にもたらす重みを考えたことがあるでしょうか。私たちに本当に喜びと満足を与えてくれるものは何なのか、今一度見直してみてはいかがでしょうか。

太字の質問はすべて、ナラティブ誘導型質問です。極論、その質問がなくても話し手の伝える内容は同じです。ただ、あえてその質問を聞き手に突き付けることで、話し手は伝えたいことを明確にし、強調することができます。こういった質問はプレゼンテーションや日常会話で最もよく使われます。書き言葉でも使えますが、「劇薬」として考えて、慎重にお使いください。書き言葉で使いすぎると、冗漫（冗長的すぎる感情的な文体）になってしまいます。

③ → 意見、スタンス、主張を表す質問

強い主張を伝える疑問文

日本語でも、「そんなことをするわけないよ！」と言う代わりに、「なんでそんなことをするんだよ？」と質問の形をとることで、否定・フラストレーション・疑問・疑いなどを表現することがあります。英語でもその手法をよく使います。

例

○ A: Did you eat my pudding?

B: **Why would I do that?** You know I hate pudding!

A：私のプリン食べた?

B：**なんで僕がそんなことするんだよ**。プリン嫌いなの知ってるだろ?

「(君も知っているとおり自分はプリンが嫌いなのに)なぜ君のプリンを盗み食いするんだよ」という質問を使って、No, I didn't. の内容にフラストレーションのニュアンスを加えて答えています。

○ A: I have the feeling I won't be able to finish my experiment by Friday.

B: You should tell the professor you are going to be late!

A: **Should I, though?** He'll be very angry, you know that. I'll give it one more day, then I'll think again.

A：金曜日までに実験を終えられそうにないよ。

B：教授に遅れそうだって言った方がいいよ!

A：**そうかなぁ**。多分怒ると思うんだ。もう 1 日様子を見て(言うかどうか)改めて考えるよ。

Should I, though? と聞くことで、本当にそうすべきか疑問であるという気持ちを表しています。

Task 1

音声を聞いて女性が意図していることは何かを選択肢の中から選びましょう。

1. 🔊 u0701

A. John will definitely be angry.

B. John's level of comprehension is low.

C. She broke John's vase.

2. 🔊 u0702

    A. She does not understand what the man means.

    B. She is worried about her job.

    C. She doesn't want to quit her job.

3. 🔊 u0703

    A. She thinks that hiking is a good idea.

    B. She is proposing an alternative way to spend the day.

    C. She is not sure it is going to rain tomorrow.

4. 🔊 u0704

    A. Her car is not new but it looks fantastic.

    B. She is actively looking for a new job.

    C. She has become able to afford a new car.

5. 🔊 u0705

    A. The man's boss has no way of knowing what happened.

    B. The boss is not going to be concerned.

    C. The man is indeed in trouble.

(Task 2)

次の文を提案や誘いを意味する疑問文として書き直してみましょう。

【例】

Let's join a cooking class together.

一緒に料理教室に行こう。

↪ **Why don't we join a cooking class together?**

    一緒に料理教室に行かない?

1.

Let's go to the movies tonight.

↻ _____

2.

We should try that new restaurant.

↻ _____

3.

We could have a picnic in the park this weekend.

↻ _____

4.

Let's take a day off and go to the beach.

↻ _____

5.

We should visit our grandparents this Sunday.

↻ _____

6.

Let's make a homemade pizza for dinner.

↻ _____

7.

We could organize a game night at our place.

↻ _____

8.

Let's go for a hike in the mountains.

↻ _____

9.

We should plan a weekend getaway.

↻ _____

10.

Let's have a barbecue party in our backyard.

↻ _____

情報の提供・追加表現

相手に情報を伝える上で、ディスコースマーカーを使って、その情報の位置づけに関するニュアンスを付加することができます。情報の提供や追加に使用するディスコースマーカーは、文章の段落の中で話の流れの方向を変えたり、文脈にニュアンス加えたりしています。こういったディスコースマーカーは発言者の判断によって使うものであり、文法事項のように「絶対ここに置かなければならない」のようなルールがあるわけではありません。

1 ― 情報の提供・追加の主なディスコースマーカー

さらに―情報を提供・追加する

> さらに、その上に、また、しかも
>
> further　　furthermore　　moreover　　what's more　　also
>
> in addition　　additionally　　on top of that　　yet another
>
> one more

○ Tanaka Industries plans to expand its operations internationally. **Further**, they aim to establish partnerships with local businesses to strengthen their position in the market.

田中産業は、国際的な事業拡大を計画しています。**さらに**、地元企業と提携して市場における地位を強化することを目指しています。

○ A study published in Medicine Today, found that regular exercise can reduce the risk of chronic disease. **Furthermore**, the study revealed that physical activity can also improve cognitive function and mental well-being.

『メディシン・トゥデイ』に掲載された研究によると、定期的な運動は慢性疾患のリスクを減らすことができます。**さらに**、運動は認知機能や精神的衛生も改善することが示されました。

○ Our online platform not only improves efficiency, but also offers advanced security features. **Moreover**, it can be customized to meet the specific needs of businesses in different industries.

当社のオンラインプラットフォームは、効率性を向上させるだけでなく、高度なセキュリティ機能も提供しています。**さらに**、様々な産業の特有のニーズに対応できるようにカスタマイズすることができます。

○ This revolutionary packaging technology significantly reduces carbon emissions. **What's more**, it can be used to reduce production costs, and thus, increase profitability.

この革新的な包装技術は、二酸化炭素の排出を大幅に削減します。**さらに**、生産コストを削減することによって利益を増やすこともできます。

○ We launched a new website to promote our face-care products. **In addition**, we introduced a loyalty program to reward regular customers.

当社は、フェイスケア製品の販売促進のため、新しいウェブサイトを立ち上げました。**さらに**、ご愛用者様への特典としてロイヤルティプログラムも導入しました。

その他のディスコースマーカー

□ another aspect　もう一つの側面、別の観点として

○ A: We found a correlation between heavy social media use and increased feelings of loneliness and depression.

B: That's definitely an important aspect to consider, but **another aspect** we should look at is the potential benefits of social media for maintaining social connections, especially in today's digital age.

A: ソーシャルメディアの多用と孤独感や抑うつ感情の増加に相関関係があることがわかりました。

B: それは確かに考慮すべき重要な側面ですが、**別の観点として**、社会的つながり、とりわけデジタル時代の今日における社会的つながりを維持するためのソーシャルメディアの潜在的な利点についても見ておく必要があります。

□ on the other hand　一方

○ The results of our experiment showed that the new drug was effective in reducing inflammation. However, **on the other hand**, it also had some side effects that need to be addressed before it can be approved for clinical use.

実験の結果、新薬が炎症を軽減する効果があることが示されました。しかし、**一方で**、臨床使用の承認に先立って対処する必要があるいくつかの副作用もありました。

○ The clients have been asking about the progress of the project, and I have scheduled a meeting with them next week to update them. **By the way**, have you looked into the budget allocation for the next quarter? We need to make sure we have enough funds to cover all the expenses.

クライアントからプロジェクトの進捗状況について問い合わせがあり、来週、報告をするためのミーティングを予定しています。**それはそうと、**来四半期の予算配分について考えてみましたか？全ての経費をカバーするのに十分な資金があるかどうか、確認する必要があります。

上記のディスコースマーカーを見て気になるのは、「さらに、また、しかも」と日本語に訳されるものが多数存在するなかで、そのすべてが自由に差し替えて使えるかどうかです。もう少し深く掘り下げてみましょう。2つのグループに分けてみます。

Further, furthermore, what's more, also, in addition, additionally, on top of that, yet another, one more などのグループと、moreover や by the way, another aspect などのグループです。

furthermore と moreover の使い分け

どちらも文の情報を追加するために使われるディスコースマーカーです。意味は似ていますが、用法にはニュアンスの違いがあります。では、furthermore と moreover を比較してみます。

まず共通点として挙げられるのは、両方とも文に情報を追加するために使用され、アイデアを接続するために使用される副詞です。また、学術的あるいはプロフェッショナルな文章でよく使用される少し硬めの表現です。昨今では、多くのネイティブ話者はその二つを同じく使ってしまっており、ニュアンスの違いが無視されがちです。しかし、正しい英語を使うという観点、とりわけ書き言葉において、その違いを意識して英語をアウトプットする方が有意義だと考えると、相違点を理解しておくメリットはあるでしょう。さて、気になる相違点を見てみましょう。

- furthermore は、**前の文をサポートまたは拡張する情報を追加**するために使われます。一方、moreover は**新しく追加される情報を紹介する**ために使用されます。
- furthermore は、話の**流れを変えずに書き続ける**(話し続ける)場合に使いますが、moreover は**予期しないポイントを紹介する**ために使用されることがあります。
- furthermore は、**関連する2つのアイデアや情報を接続したい時に使う**のが一般的です。一方、moreover は、**関連のない2つめのアイデアや情報を新たにリンクさせる**役割を担います。

○ The new policy will not only save the company money, but will also improve efficiency. **Furthermore**, it will also reduce the environmental impact of our operations.

> この新しい方針は、会社の経費節減につながるだけでなく、効率も向上させます。**さらに**、環境負荷の低減にもつながります。

この例文では、furthermore を使って、これまでの節約や効率化に関する述べたことを踏まえた情報を追加しています。furthermore は、**アイデアの論理的で自然な進行をサポート**します。moreover を見てみましょう。

○ The company's profits have increased significantly this quarter. **Moreover**, customer satisfaction ratings have also gone up.

> 今期は会社の利益が大きく伸びました。**さらに**、顧客満足度の評価も上がっています。

この例文では、moreover を使って、利益に関する前の情報とは直接関係のない、顧客満足度に関する新しい情報を紹介しています。moreover を使うことで、**新しい情報の重要性と進行中の議論との関連性が強調**されています。

どちらも追加情報を示すのに使えますが、**furthermore はアイデアの継続**を示し、**moreover は議論を補完または強化する新しいアイデアやポイントを導入**します。
この違いは微細ながら重要なものですが、発言者の"つもり"や意図次第であり、「ルール」ではないことを忘れないで使いましょう。例えば、下記の穴埋め問題をやってみてください。

The company has a great reputation for providing quality products.

_____ , their customer service is top-notch.

A. Furthermore　　　　B. Moreover

どちらを選んでも、日本語訳はいずれも「その会社は高品質の製品を提供することで良い評判を持っています。**さらに**、顧客サービスは最高レベルです」となるでしょう。furthermore を使ったら、発言者は、会社の特長を述べていくプロセスで、同一のテーマの情報を与えているというサインを出していることになります。moreover を使ったら、製品の品質というテーマから少し離れた事柄に触れているという認識であることが示されます。つまり、微細なニュアンスの違いで、どちらを使っても「正しい英語」であることに変わりありません。また、上述のように英語の多くの母語話者は、どちらも同じ意味であるかのように使っているトレンドが観察されます。

2 ─ 例と言い換えを導くディスコースマーカー

「例えば」─例を提示する表現

□ **for example**　　**for instance**　**例えば**

○ There are many ways to stay healthy. For instance, exercising regularly, eating a balanced diet, and getting enough sleep.

健康を保つ方法はたくさんあります。例えば、定期的に運動をしたり、バランスの取れた食事を摂ったり、十分な睡眠を取ったりすることです。

○ Many animals are endangered. For example, the giant panda, the Siberian tiger, and the snow leopard.

多くの動物が絶滅の危機にあります。例えば、ジャイアントパンダ、アムールトラ、ユキヒョウです。

□ such as　　like　例えば〜など、〜のような

○ There are several renewable energy sources such as solar, wind, and hydropower.

再生可能エネルギー源にはいくつかの種類があります、例えば、太陽エネルギー、風力エネルギー、水力エネルギーなどがあります。

○ There are many types of fruits like apples, oranges, and bananas.

果物には多くの種類があります、例えば、リンゴ、オレンジ、バナナなどがあります。

□ including　〜を含め、を含む

○ There are many benefits of regular exercise including improved mood, increased energy levels, and better sleep.

定期的な運動には多くの利点があります、それには気分の向上、エネルギーレベルの増加、そしてより良い睡眠が含まれます。

「〜を含め」という意味なので、厳密な例ではありませんが、何らかの主張を裏付ける例を導く際によく使われます。反復回避などより豊かな表現レパートリーを目指す上で強い味方になります。

□ namely　　in particular　　particularly
特に、はっきり言うと、具体的に言うと

○ There are three primary colors, namely, red, blue, and yellow.

3つの原色があります、それは、赤、青、黄色です。

○ Many countries, in particular those in Asia, have experienced rapid economic growth in recent years.

最近数年で、特にアジアの国々は急速な経済成長を経験しています。

□ to illustrate　例えば～に示すように

○ Many people struggle with maintaining a healthy work-life balance. To illustrate, a recent study showed that over 50% of employees feel overwhelmed by their workload and find it difficult to take time off for themselves.

多くの人々は、健康的なワークライフバランスを維持することに苦労しています。例えば、最近の研究では、50％以上の従業員が仕事の量に圧倒され、自分自身のために時間を取ることが難しいと感じていることが示されました。

□ (a) case in point　好例、代表例、典型、一例

○ Many athletes use visualization techniques to improve their performance. A case in point is Michael Phelps, who visualized his races down to the smallest detail before he even entered the pool.

多くのアスリートは、パフォーマンスを向上させるためにイメージトレーニングを使います。代表例のマイケル・フェルプスは、プールに入る前に、最も細かいところまで自らのレースをイメージしていました。

case in point は文頭、文末、文中の様々な位置で使います。

○【文頭】

A case in point is the recent study that shows a significant reduction in stress levels among people who exercise regularly.

その一例は、定期的に運動する人々の中でストレスレベルが顕著に低下していることを示す最近の研究です。

○【文末】

Despite advances in technology, there are still many areas around the world without access to the internet, and remote rural villages in developing countries are a case in point.

技術の進歩にもかかわらず、世界中でインターネットにアクセスできない地域がまだ多くあり、途上国の遠隔地の村々はその一例です。

○【文中】

Many companies are making efforts to be more environmentally friendly, with some even adopting zero-waste policies; a case in point is the XYZ Corporation, which has reduced its carbon footprint by 50% in the last five years.

多くの企業が、環境に優しい取り組みをしており、中にはゼロウェイスト方針を採用しているところの一例として、過去 5 年間でカーボンフットプリントを 50％削減した XYZ コーポレーションがあります。

□ e.g.　例えば

○ People today are adopting eco-friendly habits, e.g., using reusable bags, recycling plastic, and reducing water waste.

今日の人々がエコフレンドリーな習慣を採用しています、例えば、再利用可能なバッグを使うこと、プラスチックをリサイクルすること、水の無駄を減らすことです。

e.g. はラテン語の名残の表現で、主に書き言葉で使います。発話する場合は for example と言います。

● 言い換えの表現

□ in other words　言い換えれば

○ The film was a real bomb. In other words, it was a complete failure.

その映画は本当に駄作だった。言い換えれば、完全な失敗でした。

□ to put it another way　別の言い方をするなら

○ She felt melancholic. To put it another way, she was deeply sad.

彼女は憂鬱に感じました。別の言い方をするなら、彼女は深く悲しんでいました。

□ that is to say　that is　つまり

○ I have a tight schedule tomorrow; that is to say, I am extremely busy.

明日はスケジュールが詰まっています、つまり、私は非常に忙しいです。

□ to put it simply　simply put　簡単に言うと

○ He's not easy to get along with. To put it simply, he's a difficult person.

彼は付き合いにくいです。簡単に言うと、彼は難しい人です。

□ in a nutshell　簡潔に言うと

○ The team didn't play well; in a nutshell, they were awful.

チームはうまくプレイしなかった、簡潔に言うと、彼らはひどかった。

□ to sum up　要約すると

○ The meal was expensive and the service was terrible. To sum up, it was a disappointing experience.

食事は高価で、サービスはひどかった。要約すると、それは失望する経験でした。

□ i.e.　すなわち

○ He will start his new job next week, i.e., on the first Monday of September.

彼は来週、新しい仕事を始めます、すなわち、9月の最初の月曜日に。

i.e. も、e.g. 同様ラテン語表現の名残で、主に書き言葉で使います。発話する場合は、in other words あるいは that is と言います。

文を完成させる最適な選択肢を選びましょう。

1.

The data collected in this study indicate that exercise can improve cognitive function. Moreover, _____.

    A. it was also found to have a positive impact on mood.

    B. other experts in the field have expressed concerns regarding the quality of the data.

    C. 25% of the participants reported disruption in sleep.

2.

This report presents an analysis of the company's financial performance for the last quarter. In addition, _____.

    A. the report also includes a breakdown of the sales figures by product category.

    B. the report highlights the importance of teamwork for achieving success in the workplace.

    C. the report details the skills one has to develop in order to become a successful CEO.

3.

This article discusses the benefits of meditation for mental health. By the way, _____.

    A. the article also provides some tips for beginners on how to start a meditation practice.

    B. I read in another article that meditation is also very helpful for improving concentration and productivity.

    C. the article argues that meditation is not suitable for everyone and can have some negative effects.

4.

David's presentation outlined the main features of the new software program our company released last month. What's more, _____.

    A. he also included a demo of the software in action.

    B. the presentation discussed the history of software development and its future prospects.

    C. David has developed an impressive skillset as a salesperson.

5.

Muramoto's new novel explores the themes of love and loss in a unique and engaging way. Another aspect of the novel _____.

    A. that deserves attention is its use of humor to lighten the mood.

    B. is that its first edition sold out in a mere two weeks.

    C. is that I did not enjoy it very much.

Unit 9

対照・否定表現

ディスコースマーカーは、対照的な情報や否定の表現でも重要な役割を担います。ここでは、対照・否定表現がもつ意味の違いや語順のバリエーションを整理します。

対照・否定のディスコースマーカーは、発言者の話の流れを転換させるもので、ナラティブに起承転結をもたらします。聞き手や読み手にとって情報が消化しやすくなり、面白みや深みが増します。本 Unit では、誰でも使ったことがある but や however に加えて、アウトプットのレパートリーを広げてより成熟度の高い発言を目指していきましょう。

1 ─ 対照・否定を表現する主なディスコースマーカー

but	however	in contrast	nevertheless	even so
still	conversely	on the contrary	nonetheless	yet
whereas	though	although	even though	instead
despite	regardless	notwithstanding	in spite of	

これらは、2 つの考えや発言の間の対比や矛盾を示すために使われることが多いディスコースマーカーです。アイデア間の関係を明確にし、発言者の伝えたいニュアンスを読み手や聞き手に明確に伝えるのに役立ちます。

but　しかし、だが

教科書や文法書によっては、but は文の中でしか使ってはいけないというルールがあると教えられています。しかし、実際の英語では文頭に使われることがよくあります。口語のみならず一定の書き言葉でも許される使い方です。書き言葉の中でも、学術論文や契約書など「硬い」文体では依然として文頭に使うことは避けられており、報道や文学なら文頭の but が散見されます。

○ We wanted to go to the zoo **but** it started raining, so we decided to stay home.

動物園に行きたかったのですが、雨が降り始めたので、家にいることにしました。

○ We had planned to go to the zoo on Sunday. **But** we ended up staying home because it started raining.

日曜日は動物園に行く予定でした。が、雨が降り始めたので結局家にいることにしました。

however　しかし、けれども、しかしながら、また一方

○ The company has seen great success in recent years. **However**, this quarter's earnings report was disappointing.

同社は近年、大きな成功を収めています。しかし、今期の決算報告には失望させられました。

このような文であれば、however の代わりに but を使っても差し支えません。同じ表現を使いすぎないように、but と however を使いわけることをおすすめします。

上記の例文のように、however は多くの場合文頭に使います。しかし、文中にカンマで挿入して使うこともあります。

○ From the report, I understood that the company is in decent financial health. The language of the report, **however**, felt biased towards showing only the bright side.

報告書から、会社が財務的に健全であることが理解できました。しかし、報告書の言葉は、明るい面ばかりに偏っているように感じられました。

上記の例文では、however を but に差し替えることができません。but を使うには、構文を変える必要があります。

○ From the report, I understood that the company is in decent financial health. **But** the language of the report felt biased towards showing only the bright side.

その報告書からは、会社はまずまずの財務状態にあることがわかります。ただし、報告書の言葉遣いは明るい面だけを示している傾向があるように感じました。

また、however は同時に「どんなに〜、どれほど〜でも」を意味する副詞でもあり、対照・否定でない意味でも使われます。

○ However hard I study, I still struggle with math.

どんなに勉強しても、数学は苦手なんです。

in contrast　一方、対照的に

○ The current CEO's management style is very hands-off. In contrast, her predecessor was very hands-on and got involved in every aspect of the business.

現 CEO の経営スタイルは、非常に手離れが良いのです。一方、前任者は非常に現場主義で、ビジネスのあらゆる側面に関与していました。

nevertheless, nonetheless, still, yet, even so
〜にもかかわらず、〜にしても、〜とは言え、〜とは言うものの

これらを類語と見なし、使っていきましょう。【in spite of + 名詞・句】などとは異なり、名詞、句、節と組み合わせることができません。

Mrs. Johnson was a very strict teacher. The students loved her nonetheless. という文を in spite of を使って書き直すと、以下のようになります。

○ Mrs. Johnson was a very strict teacher. **In spite of** that (in spite of her being very strict), the students loved her.

Mrs. Johnson は非常に厳格な教師でした。それにも関わらず、生徒たちは彼女が好きでした。

○ The company faced significant setbacks in the past year, including a major product recall and a decline in market share. **Nevertheless**, the company's new CEO was able to turn things around by implementing a bold new strategy focused on innovation and customer satisfaction.

同社は昨年、大規模な製品回収や市場シェアの低下など、大きな挫折に直面しました。**それでもなお**、同社の新 CEO は、イノベーションと顧客満足に焦点を当てた大胆な新戦略を実行することで、状況を好転させることができました。

○ Our team's research findings were challenged by a rival group in the scientific community. **Nonetheless**, we were able to defend our findings and provide additional evidence to support our claims.

我々のチームの研究結果は学界のライバルグループによって疑問視されました。**それでも**、私たちは研究結果を守り、主張を裏付けるための追加の証拠を提供することができました。

○ The demand for electric vehicles has grown rapidly in recent years, prompting several major car manufacturers to invest heavily in this market. **Still**, there are concerns among consumers about the limited range and accessibility of charging stations, which could limit the widespread adoption of EVs.

電気自動車の需要は近年急速に伸びており、複数の大手自動車メーカーがこの市場に多額の投資を行うようになりました。**それでも**、消費者の間では、走行距離の制約や充電スタンドの利用しにくさのせいで、電気自動車の普及には限界があるのではないかという懸念があります。

○ The pharmaceutical company has invested heavily in research and development to create a new drug to treat a rare disease. **Yet**, the drug is still to receive regulatory approval, and there are concerns about its safety and efficacy.

製薬会社は、希少疾病を治療するための新薬を生み出すために、研究開発に多額の投資をしてきました。**そうとは言え**、その薬はまだ規制当局の承認を得ておらず、その安全性と有効性に懸念があります。

○ The scientific experiment did not yield the expected results, casting doubt on the validity of the initial hypothesis. **Even so**, the researchers remained determined to uncover the underlying factors and conducted further investigations to refine their understanding.

実験は期待通りの結果を得られず、当初の仮説の妥当性が疑われました。**それでも**、研究者たちはその原因を明らかにするためにさらに調査を重ね、理解を深めていきました。

though, although, even though　～にもかかわらず、しかし

3つとも同じ意味ですが、構文（語順）やコロケーション（組み合わせ）など使い方に違いが見られます。また、although は though に比べて若干フォーマルな感じが出ますので、書き言葉の文頭やより硬い表現と組み合わせる傾向があります。

例 【文頭に使う場合】

○ Although (= though) I worked day and night, I still couldn't finish in time.

昼夜問わず働いたにもかかわらず、期限内に終了することができませんでした。

これは、I worked day and night, but I still couldn't finish in time. とまったく同じです。「にもかからず」を強調したい場合、although や though を使った方が良いです。

例 【文中に使う場合】

○ I can't run a full marathon, **though** I run every day.

= I can't run a full marathon **although** I run every day.

= I run every day, **but** I can't run a full marathon.

私は毎日走っているけれども、フルマラソンは走れません。

例 【文末に使う場合】

○ I'm tired of studying for the exam. It wasn't as hard as I imagined, **though**.

試験勉強に疲れました。でも、想像していたほど難しくはありませんでした。

文末には、although や but は使いません。

conversely, in contrast, on the contrary
逆に、反対に、逆に言うと、それと違って、～と対照的に

○ She thought that studying more would lead to better grades. **Conversely**, it resulted in increased stress and lower academic performance.

彼女は勉強したら成績が上がると思っていたのに、逆にストレスが増えて成績が下がってしまいました。

○ The company's competitors focused on aggressive marketing tactics to gain market share. **In contrast**, our company relied on product quality and customer satisfaction as our primary strategies.

競合他社は、市場シェアを獲得するために積極的なマーケティング戦術に重点を置いていました。**それと対照的に**、当社は製品の品質と顧客満足を主要な戦略としていました。

○ Many people believe that success brings happiness. **Conversely**, research suggests that happiness often leads to greater success in various areas of life.

多くの人は、成功は幸福をもたらすと信じています。**反対に**、研究によると、幸せは人生のさまざまな領域でより大きな成功をもたらすことが多いようです。

○ The popular opinion is that technology has made people more isolated. On the contrary, technology has provided new ways to connect and communicate with others around the world.

テクノロジーは人々をより孤立させるというものだとよく言われています。**まったく逆で**、テクノロジーは、世界中の人とつながり、コミュニケーションをとるための新しい方法を提供しています。

● in contrast と on the contrary の違い

両方とも「反対に、逆に、〜と対照的に」などの意味で使いますが、その違いを理解して正しく使い分けることが重要です。意味合い的に同じカテゴリに属しても、差し替えて使うと間違いになるので注意が必要です。

・**on the contrary** は前に来ている発言と対照的な発言を導きます。

・**in contrast** は、前後に紹介する違ったアプローチやアイデアを読み手に(聞き手)に見分けてもらうために使います。

また、in contrast に with や to で続けて名詞や名詞句と繋げることができますが、on the contrary はそういった使い方はできません。

例

○ Many people assume that eating fats is always unhealthy. **On the contrary**, there are good fats that are essential for a balanced diet.

多くの人々は、脂肪を摂取することは常に健康に悪いと思っています。ところが逆で、バランスの取れた食事に欠かせない良い脂肪もあります。

on the contrary を使って、前の発言を否定しています。この文では、in contrast は使えません。

例

○ The team worked diligently on their project and achieved remarkable results. Their competitors, **in contrast**, lacked the same level of dedication.

そのチームはプロジェクトに熱心に取り組んで顕著な成果を上げました。それに対し、彼らの競合他社は同じレベルの献身を欠いていました。

ここでは、in contrast を使って、その前に来ている発言を否定しているわけではなく、対照的な状況を描写しているから on the contrary は使えません。

whereas 一方で、ところが、であるのに対して

二つのものや人などを対比させつつ、否定・肯定ではなく、異なる側面や見方を紹介するディスコースマーカーです。

例

○ Both companies A and B have been very successful financially. Company A focuses primarily on cost reduction, **whereas** Company B emphasizes product innovation and differentiation to gain a competitive advantage.

A社もB社も財務的に大成功しています。A社は主にコスト削減に重点を置いている**一方で**、B社は競争優位を得るために製品の革新と差別化に重点を置いています。

○ The marketing department prefers traditional advertising channels to reach a broader audience, **whereas** the sales team relies heavily on digital marketing strategies targeting specific customer segments.

マーケティング部門は、より多くの人々にリーチするために従来の広告チャネルを好む**一方で**、営業チームは特定の顧客層をターゲットにしたデジタルマーケティング戦略に大きく賭けています。

instead (of) 〜の代わり、それよりむしろ、そうしないで、その代わりに

instead of は名詞や節（名詞節、動名詞節）と一緒に使います。

○ I'm on a diet, so **instead of** bread, I eat tofu.

ダイエット中なので、パンの**代わりに**豆腐を食べています。

○ **Instead of** going for my usual morning run, I'll do squats today.

いつもの朝ランの**代わりに**、今日はスクワットにしよう。

of なしの instead は、動詞や動詞句と組み合わせて使い、同じく「代わりに」を意味します。

○ We were going to eat Italian but we opted for Chinese instead (= instead of Italian).

私たちはイタリアンを食べるつもりでしたが、代わりに中華料理にしました。

○ I wanted to go to Kenya. But instead, I went to Morocco.

ケニアに行きたかったのですが、代わりにモロッコに行きました。

despite, in spite of, regardless (of), notwithstanding
〜に（も）かかわらず、〜を顧みず

notwithstanding を除き、despite, in spite of, regardless (of) はよく the fact（〜の事実にもかかわらず）と組み合わせて使われます。

例

○ **Despite** the fact that the economy is experiencing a downturn, the tech sector has shown some impressive growth.

経済が停滞しているにもかかわらず、IT 産業は目覚ましい成長を見せています。

○ **In spite of** significant scientific advancements, there are still many unanswered questions about the nature of dark matter.

相当の科学的進歩にもかかわらず、暗黒物質の本質についてはまだ多くの未解決の問いがあります。

○ The fact that inflation is on the rise hasn't deterred consumers from making large purchases, **despite** economic uncertainties.

インフレが進んでいる中、消費者は経済の不確定性を抱えながらも大きな買い物をすることに躊躇がありません。

○ **In spite of** the fact that technological innovations have revolutionized the healthcare industry, access to quality healthcare remains a challenge in certain regions.

技術革新が医療業界に変革をもたらしてきたにもかかわらず、一部の地域では質の高い医療へのアクセスが依然として課題となっています。

○ Scientists have not yet discovered a definitive cure for certain types of cancer, **in spite of** remarkable progress in understanding the disease.

がんの一部のタイプについては、病気の理解における驚くべき進展にもかかわらず、まだ決定的な治療法は見つかっていません。

○ **Regardless** of their social background, all students should have equal access to quality education to foster scientific progress and innovation.

社会的背景**にかかわらず**、すべての生徒が科学の進歩と革新を促進するために、質の高い教育を平等に受けることができるようにすべきです。

○ **Notwithstanding** the challenges faced by the economy, society, and businesses during the pandemic, innovative entrepreneurs found ways to adapt and thrive in the digital landscape.

パンデミック中に経済、社会、ビジネスが直面した課題にもかかわらず、革新的な起業家たちはデジタルの世界で適応し、繁栄する方法を見つけました。

(Task 1)

音声を聞き、会話を完成させるのに最も自然な選択肢を選びましょう。

1. 🔊) u0901

    A. We should go instead.

    B. We should go regardless.

    C. Conversely, we should go.

2. 🔊) u0902

    A. We know a lot about the Egyptian ones, whereas we are just starting to explore the ones in Mexico.

    B. Despite the fact that the Mayan pyramids are in Mexico, the Egyptian ones are in Egypt.

    C. Nevertheless, we went to see the pyramids in Egypt.

3. 🔊) u0903

    A. I'm not a huge fan of sushi, though.

    B. Yes, we should go to Tim's party instead.

    C. He's our friend, we should go regardless.

4. 🔊) u0904

    A. In contrast, I really like this house.

    B. Still, I'm not convinced it's worth investing so much money.

    C. I've lived there for a long time, though.

5. 🔊 u0905

    A. However, I have never met her.

    B. On the contrary, I think she's lovely.

    C. Yet they say she is a very difficult person.

6. 🔊 u0906

    A. Regardless of all of that, I don't date sporty guys.

    B. Furthermore, he also runs very fast.

    C. I really enjoy playing baseball, however.

7. 🔊 u0907

    A. Although I tried, I couldn't get much sleep yesterday.

    B. Thank you so much. Yet another reason to upgrade my smartphone.

    C. I'm sorry. But I was with a client.

⬤ Task 2 ⬤

各パッセージの空所を埋めましょう。

1. 🔊 u0908

The company's revenues have been steadily increasing, but expenses have also been on the rise. Thus, ⁽¹⁾_____ the increase in revenues, the company's profit margins have been declining.

    A. despite

    B. although

    C. instead

⁽²⁾_____ , the company has implemented cost-saving measures to offset the impact of rising expenses.

    A. Nevertheless

    B. However

    C. Notwithstanding

(3)_____ , competitors in the market have managed to maintain higher profit margins by optimizing their operational costs.

    A. Furthermore

    B. In spite of

    C. In contrast

(4)_____ the company's strong brand presence and loyal customer base have helped mitigate the effects of the declining profit margins.

    A. Nevertheless

    B. Whereas

    C. Despite

2. ◀) u0909

Our university's research team has made significant progress in cancer treatment.

(1)_____ , the experimental drug has shown promising results in shrinking tumor sizes in early-stage clinical trials.

    A. On the contrary

    B. Nevertheless

    C. On top of that

(2)_____ breakthrough in the field of oncology is the development of personalized treatment plans based on genetic profiling.

    A. Despite

    B. Yet another

    C. Still

(3)_____ exciting development is the use of immunotherapy, which harnesses the body's immune system to fight cancer cells.

    A. One more

    B. On the contrary

    C. In spite of

(4)_____ , the research team is exploring the potential of targeted therapy to minimize side effects and improve patient outcomes.

    A. Moreover

    B. However

    C. Whereas

3. ◀)) u0910

Clark's findings support the effectiveness of traditional teaching methods, (1)_____ technology is rapidly advancing.

    A. even though

    B. even

    C. further

(2)_____ , incorporating technology into education has its advantages, such as enhancing student engagement and providing interactive learning experiences.

    A. Even though

    B. Even so

    C. Notwithstanding

(3)_____ , many educators prefer traditional teaching methods due to their proven track record of success.

    A. Moreover

    B. Still

    C. Additionally

(4)_____ , some argue that technology should be embraced in the classroom to prepare students for the digital age.

    A. Furthermore

    B. Conversely

    C. In spite of

4. 🔊) u0911

Recent studies have shown the benefits of regular exercise on mental health.

(1)_____ improving mental well-being, exercise has been linked to increased productivity at work.

   A. In addition to

   B. Despite the fact that

   C. Moreover

(2)_____ , it has been found to enhance cognitive function, leading to better decision-making skills.

   A. Conversely

   B. Furthermore

   C. However

(3)_____ , engaging in physical activity can also help reduce stress levels and promote overall work-life balance.

   A. Moreover

   B. Regardless

   C. Despite

(4)_____ , incorporating exercise into one's routine has been shown to boost creativity and enhance problem-solving abilities.

   A. Conversely

   B. Furthermore

   C. Still

対照・否定表現

参照と言い換え ①

英語では、一般的に繰り返しは推奨されません。話し言葉でも書き言葉でも、同じ人や物や現象に何度も言及する必要がある場合、別な表現に言い換えることが望ましいとされています。そのため、英語には繰り返しを避けるための様々な手法があります。

専門用語に代表される何らかの特殊な用語については、読み手の理解に混乱を来さないように言い換えずそのまま使うといった、繰り返しが推奨される例外的な内容もあります。こうした一部の例外を除けば、繰り返しを避ける努力は大いに評価の対象です。ロジカルで美しいアウトプットのためには、各種の参照表現や豊富なボキャブラリーをフルに活用していくこと重要です。

参照表現や言い換えは繰り返しを避けるために存在する主な手法ですが、言い換えを優先するあまり読み手の理解を損なってはいけません。意味が明確であり、聞き手や読み手が問題なく理解できる状況に限って使うことが許されるということです。同義語や語彙の定義を利用するだけでなく、「参照表現」を使いこなすことも重要です。

繰り返しを避けて、簡潔かつエレガントな表現を目指しましょう。

1 ● 参照表現

代名詞と指示語

反復回避の最も一般的な方法は、人物、物、場所、概念など発言の対象を代名詞で置き換えることです。日本語では、通常は代名詞を必要最低限しか使いません。「私は」「彼は」などで始まる文は日本語としてはあまり美しく聞こえず、不自然な印象を与えがちなのがその理由です。対照的に、英語はふんだんに代名詞を使います。代名詞によって同じ語の繰り返しを避けたすっきりと簡潔な文を、理解しやすい表現として評価する傾向があるからです。

☐ Pronouns 代名詞: **it, she, he, we, they**
☐ Possessive Pronouns 所有代名詞:
　its, his, her, hers, our, our, their, theirs
☐ Objective Pronouns 目的格の代名詞: **him, her, it, us, them**
☐ Demonstrative Pronouns 指示代名詞: **this, these, that, those**
☐ Reference Phrases 参照フレーズ:
　the first, the second, the former, the latter, the last

○ 良くない例

Dr. Patterson will present Dr. Patterson's research at the conference. Dr. Patterson has been preparing for his presentation at the conference for months.

○ 改善案

Dr. Patterson will present his research at the conference. He has been preparing for this for months.

パターソン博士は会議で自身の研究を発表します。彼はこれの準備を数か月間してきました。

His は Dr. Patterson のことを指し、his research は Dr. Patterson's research であり、this は his presentation at the conference を指すことが明らかです。

○ 良くない例

The company is considering a merger or an acquisition. The company feels a merger would be a strategic move, but an acquisition could also be beneficial.

○ 改善案

The company is considering a merger or an acquisition. <u>The former</u> would be a strategic move, while <u>the latter</u> could also prove beneficial.

その企業は合併または買収を検討しています。前者は戦略的な動きとなるでしょうが、後者もまた有益であることが証明されるかもしれません。

ここでは、the former は merger（合併）、the latter は acquisition（吸収）であり、文におけるそれぞれの位置を参考に繰り返しを避けています。

繰り返しを避けるために各種の代名詞や参照フレーズを使いますが、その使い方を誤ると、読み手の理解を損ねてしまうことがあります。代名詞や参照フレーズを使う場合は何を指すか明確な状況に限って使うことが極めて重要です。良くない例とその改善されたバージョンを見てみましょう。

○ 良くない例

Emily met with the CEO and the marketing manager, Sarah. <u>She</u> told her that the company's profits have been declining.

この使い方だと、she と her は誰のことを指すかが不明瞭です。

例

○ 改善案①

Emily met with the CEO and the marketing manager, Sarah. Emily informed <u>Sarah</u> that the company's profits have been declining.

エミリーは CEO とマーケティングマネージャーのサラと会いました。エミリーはサラに会社の利益が減少していると伝えました。

○ 改善案②

Emily met with the CEO and the marketing manager, Sarah. Emily informed <u>them</u> that the company's profits have been declining.

エミリーは CEO とマーケティングマネージャーのサラと会いました。エミリーは彼らに会社の利益が減少していると伝えました。

(Task 1)

ボックス内の代名詞や参照フレーズを使って、空所を埋めましょう。

□ 代名詞 **it**, **she**, **he**, **we**, **they**

□ 所有代名詞 **its**, **his**, **her**, **hers**, **our**, **our**, **their**, **theirs**

□ 目的格の代名詞 **him**, **her**, **it**, **us**, **them**

□ 指示代名詞 **this**, **these**, **that**, **those**

□ 参照フレーズ **the first**, **the second**, **the former**, **the latter**, **the last**

1.

Do you know that honeybees play a crucial role in pollination? Over the last few decades, _____ numbers have sharply declined, raising concerns about _____ future survival.

2.

The board had two important decisions to make: invest in research and development, or initiate a stock buyback program. _____ was seen as an investment in the future, while _____ was a way to immediately reward shareholders.

3.

The CEO and the CFO had a detailed discussion about the company's financial health. _____ shared _____ concerns about the rising operational costs.

4.

When Lucy discovered the lost manuscript in the library, _____ felt like she had found a hidden treasure. _____ knew _____ value was immense.

5.

The architect and the builder had a debate about the design of the house. _____ argued for a modern design, while _____ preferred a more traditional approach. In the end, _____ decided to ask Jack, the owner of the house, about _____ preference.

6.

William Shakespeare didn't go to university. However, after _____ schooling, _____ wrote some of the most celebrated works in the English language.

7.

The human body has millions of neurons. _____ transmit information between different parts of the body, playing a crucial role in _____ ability to sense and respond to the environment.

8.

After a long meeting, the marketing team and the sales team finally reached a consensus. _____ decided to jointly launch a new campaign, with _____ focusing on online promotions and _____ focusing on direct customer engagement.

─────────────── (Task 2) ───────────────

ボックス内の代名詞や参照フレーズを使って、直前の太字を言い換える語を空所に入れましょう。

□ 代名詞 **it**, **she**, **he**, **we**, **they**
□ 所有代名詞 **its**, **his**, **her**, **hers**, **our**, **our**, **their**, **theirs**
□ 目的格の代名詞 **him**, **her**, **it**, **us**, **them**
□ 指示代名詞 **this**, **these**, **that**, **those**
□ 参照フレーズ **the first**, **the second**, **the former**, **the latter**, **the last**

In the mid-1940s, Chester Carlson, a patent attorney with a knack for engineering, found himself exhausted with the manual process of producing multiple copies of documents. This struggle inspired **Carlson** (_____) to experiment in **Carlson's** (_____) kitchen, leading to a revolutionary invention that we now know as the photocopier.

Carlson's (_____) first attempts were unsuccessful. Using static electricity, **Carlson** (_____) tried to attract dry particles of ink onto a piece of paper, but **the attempt** (_____) resulted in a mess. Yet, **Carlson** (_____) was not deterred. He persisted, recognizing the potential of **Carlson's** (_____) concept. His latter attempts included a more refined version of **Carlson's** (_____) initial strategy. This time, **Carlson** (_____) succeeded in creating a legible copy of a text on a slide. **Carlson** (_____) called the process "xerography", derived from the Greek words for "dry" and "writing".

However, the journey of transforming **Carlson's** (_____) invention into a commercial product was challenging. **Carlson** (_____) struggled to find a company willing to invest in **the invention** (_____) The first 20 firms he approached rejected **Carlson's** (_____) proposal, unable to see the potential. Eventually, the Haloid Company, later known as Xerox, decided to take a risk and backed his idea. The Haloid Company's (_____) gamble paid off, and the photocopier became a cornerstone of the modern office.

The impact of Carlson's invention was profound. **The invention** (_____) transformed the dynamics of paperwork, enabling businesses to reproduce documents quickly and efficiently. In spite of the initial hurdles, **Carlson's** (_____) determination led to a breakthrough that has left its mark on our daily lives.

参照と言い換え ②

すでに扱った「参照表現」に加え、様々な言い換え表現が存在します。Unit 10 では、繰り返しを避けた簡潔でエレガントな語りのために、さまざまな代名詞を使用しました。この Unit では、言い換えや繰り返しを避けるための他のアプローチに焦点を当てます。これらのテクニックは、日常会話から学術的な議論まで幅広く応用できます。学会での質疑応答、職場でのやりとりやミーティング、文章を書くときなど、英語でコミュニケーションをとらなければならないあらゆる場面で役立ちます。

1 語義、語釈、定義

説明でボキャブラリーに立体感をもたせる

何かを説明する時や、正確な言葉がわからないときに、定義を使って表現します。言葉で何かを定義したり説明したりする方法はたくさんありますが、ここでは簡単な公式を紹介します。語彙のカテゴリを定め、その用途、存在する場所、または、何らかの詳細(特徴)を述べる順番が一般的です。例を見てみましょう。

word	category	application / location / details
a pencil	is a tool	used for writing
a grant	is a sum of money	used for scientific research
a beach	is an area of sand	next to the sea
a PhD	is an advanced academic degree	given to doctoral researchers after they defend their dissertation
an axe	is a tool	used for cutting wood
sadness	is a state of mind	in which people are unhappy
influenza	is an illness	characterized by high temperature
earlobes	are the soft tissue	located at the bottom of the ear

特定の語彙を繰り返さず、その「定義」の一部を言い換え表現として使うことによって簡潔でエレガントな英語の表現ができます。

 例

○ 良くない例

Tom received a PhD. The PhD propelled his academic career.

トムは博士号を取得しました。その博士号が彼の学術的なキャリアを推進しました。

○ 改善案

Tom received a PhD. The <u>advanced degree</u> propelled his academic career.

トムは博士号を受け取りました。その高度な学位が彼の学術的なキャリアを推進しました。

○ 良くない例

I went to the beach yesterday. Spending time at the beach helped me clear my head.

昨日、私はビーチに行きました。ビーチで過ごすことは、私の頭を整理するのに役立ちました。

○ 改善案

I went to the beach yesterday. Spending time <u>near the sea</u> helped me clear my head.

昨日、私はビーチに行きました。海の近くで過ごすことが、私の頭を整理するのに役立ちました。

2 ── 類語、同義語、反対語

言い換えのバリエーションを広げる

繰り返しを避けるというテーマにおいて、類語と反対語は極めて重要な存在です。英語は他の言語に比べて多くの言語の影響を受けており、長い歴史の中で、ノルド語やラテン語、10世紀以降中フランス語など様々な言語からボキャブラリーを受け入れてきています。英語が有数の豊富なボキャブラリーと豊かな表現力を持っているのは、こうした背景によるものです。類語と反対語を使ってどんどん言い換えを好む言語になったのも、ひょっ

とするとそういった歴史的な背景から派生した文化なのかもしれません。その反面、同じような意味を持つ数多くの語彙が存在することにより、学習者に大きなチャレンジを突き付けているとも言えます。

同義語と類語は、類似または同一の意味を持つ語で、反対語は、反対の意味を持つ語です。英語の学習をしていく上で、同義語と反対語で常に語彙を増やすことは非常に重要であり、有用です。類語・反対語の豊かさは教養ある大人の特徴の一つです。書き言葉はもちろんのこと、会話においても気転の効いた流れを作るには強い味方になってくれます。普段の学習において新しい単語と出会った際に、その類語や反対語も併せて調べて覚えておくと立体感のある語彙力が形成されます。

ただし、同義語や類語はすべて同じように使われるとは限りません。同義語であっても使い方が違う場合や、入れ替えが不可能な場合もあるため、使用する際には注意が必要です。いくつかの例を見てみましょう。

○ You must **follow** the rules. = You must **observe** the rules.
= You must **abide by** the rules.

follow、observe と abide by は同じく使える類語です。しかし、by をつけないで abide だけで使ってしまうと「住まう」というまったく異なる意味になってしまいます。
plummet、plunge と dive は「急激に減る」という意味においては類語ですが、dive は潜るスポーツの「ダイビング」を指すこともあり、plummet と plunge にはその意味が存在しません。

③ 再話、要約

自分の言葉で語り直す

読んだ小説や鑑賞した映画を友達にざっくり伝える場面を想像すると、内容を咀嚼して、あらすじを自分の言葉で伝えることが必要になります。その過程を指す用語として本書では「再話」を使っています。マイナーなポイントを無視して、内容の要点を「語り直す」といった「要約」とも言える行為です。重要な点とマイナーな点を特定して、残す内容と削ぎ落

す内容を決めるという判断は大切ですが、ここでは、再話の言葉選びに焦点を当てたいと思います。要約して内容を概念化するには、類語や反対語、そして前述の定義は、再話をするときに使える便利なツールです。しかし、最終的には新しい文章を考えなければなりません。その際、一般的には、パッセージ全体の一文一文を再現することを目指すのではなく、最も重要な情報を要約し、自分の言葉で伝えることが肝要です。それでは、Task 3 の最初のストーリーがどのように要約されているかを見ていきます。これを例にして、他のパッセージも同じように再話することにしましょう。

○【パッセージ】

In the early 19th century, a British chemist named John Walker accidentally stumbled upon an extraordinary invention that would revolutionize fire-starting forever: the friction match. In 1826, while stirring a mixture of chemicals in his lab, Walker noticed a dried lump on the end of his stick. Without realizing it, he had just created the first friction match. Walker's invention consisted of a wooden splint coated with chemicals that ignited when struck against a rough surface. This simple but groundbreaking discovery provided a convenient and reliable way to start fires, and it soon spread across the world, changing the way people lit up their lives.

○【要約】

John Walker, a chemist, accidentally discovered the friction match in 1826. This simple invention consisted of a wooden splint coated with ignitable chemicals that ignited when struck on a rough surface. The match revolutionized fire-starting and quickly gained popularity worldwide, changing how people lit up their lives.

元来のストーリーは 100 語程度ですが、要約は 50 語弱です。しかし、読んでわかるように、重要なポイントは押さえてあります。再話の際に以下のことを意識しておきましょう。

・再話をする上で削ぎ落す内容を決めます。削ると全体図が伝わらないものは残して、削っても影響が少ないあるいはないものを削りましょう。

・段落は話の論理的な塊です。長い文章であれば、おそらく丸ごと削っても全体図が伝わる段落もあるでしょう。その段階を経て生き残った段落を段落ごとに要約していきます。その時は、「削るか・残すか」の判断だけでやると素っ気ない文体になりがちなので、段落全体の意味を考えて別の言葉で伝えます。ここは、類語・反対語の知識が問われる場面です。

・アカデミックな文章であれば、再話をする人の意見やスタンスへの言及は極力避けるべきですが、一般の文章（例：映画や小説のあらすじ）であれば、若干のバイアスが入っても良いでしょう。多少の「独断と偏見」が、ストーリーを短くしても臨場感ある再話のスパイスとなることもよくあります。

• (Task 1) •

表にある語彙の定義を書いてみましょう。解答編には模範解答が掲載されていますが、気にせず自分の言葉で定義を書いてみましょう。

word	category	application / location / details
pipette		
engine		
hammer		
CAD software		
petri dish		
helium		
bulldozer		
gravity		
optical mouse		
steam roller		
seminar		
chess		

下記の語彙から各文の下線部分の代わりに使える類語を選びましょう。

thrive   inquire   conscientious   business
caught a glimpse of   loathe

1.

I absolutely <u>despise</u> the taste of mushrooms.

2.

Sally is a(n) <u>diligent</u> student who always completes her assignments on time.

3.

The company plans to expand its <u>operations</u> to other countries.

4.

Under favorable conditions, the business is likely to <u>flourish</u> and generate significant profits.

5.

As I walked by the window, I <u>saw</u> the magnificent sunset.

6.

If you have any questions, feel free to <u>ask</u> the instructor after the class.

下記のパッセージを要約した文を選択肢から選びましょう。要約に必要なのは「重要なポイント」であり、不要なのは「マイナーなポイント」です。その見分けをする練習です。

In the late 20th century, a transformative invention emerged that would forever change the way we connect, communicate, and access information: the Internet. Originating from the Advanced Research Projects Agency Network (ARPANET) in the 1960s, the Internet was initially developed as a decentralized communication network to withstand a nuclear attack.

Over time, the Internet expanded beyond its military and academic roots, becoming a global network of interconnected computers. In 1989, Tim Berners-Lee invented the World Wide Web, introducing hyperlinks that allowed easy access and navigation of information.
The 1990s witnessed the commercialization of the Internet, with the establishment of Internet service providers (ISPs) and the creation of user-friendly web browsers like Netscape Navigator and Internet Explorer. This commercialization opened up the Internet to a broader audience and paved the way for its widespread adoption.

The Internet connected people worldwide, transcending geographical boundaries and revolutionizing communication, collaboration, and the sharing of knowledge. Technological advancements followed suit, with the development of search engines, email, e-commerce platforms, social media, and streaming services.

Today, the Internet is an integral part of our daily lives, empowering us with instant access to information, enabling seamless communication across continents, and fostering a global community.

【要約】
書き出しの文：
The invention of the Internet revolutionized global communication and information access.

1. 2 つ目の文を次の A 〜 C から選びましょう。

    A. From its military origins, the Internet expanded into a worldwide network, leading to the invention of the World Wide Web and its commercialization.

    B. The Advanced Research Projects Agency Network (ARPANET) was the starting point of the Internet in the 1960s.

    C. Tim Berners-Lee, who invented hyperlinks, set the stage for the expansion of the World Wide Web, or what we commonly refer to as the Internet nowadays.

3 つ目の文 :

The Internet connected people globally, facilitating collaboration and knowledge sharing.

2. 4 つ目の文を次の A 〜 C から選びましょう。

    A. The launch of Internet service providers established the infrastructure on which the Internet grew and is thriving today.

    B. Technological advancements, such as search engines, email, e-commerce, social media, and streaming services, further transformed the Internet's capabilities.

    C. Many predicted that the advent of the Internet would mean the end of libraries, but today we can clearly see that this prediction did not materialize.

間接話法 ①

私たちは、他者とコミュニケーションをとるときに、自分の考え、ニーズ、懸念、感情を相手と共有したいと思うようにできています。また、自分や他の人に他者が何を伝えているのか、とても気になります。このようなコミュニケーションには、言語的なもの(話す、書く)、非言語的なもの(ボディランゲージ、表情、姿勢、ジェスチャー、物音、行動)があります。誰かが自分や他の人にしたこと、言ったことを他の誰かと共有するとき、私たちは報告をしています。一般的に 2 つの方法で報告し、しばしばこれらを互いに混在させます。

1 ● 直接話法または引用話法

そのままの言葉で伝える

誰かの口から出た、誰かに向けられた正確な言葉を(話したり書いたりして)伝える場合です。直接話法は、一般的に、できるだけ正確に(全く同じ言葉を、そのまま)伝えなければならない場面で使われます。諺や格言のようなものはもちろん直接話法しか使いません。引用符で囲って誰かの発言を論文などで伝える、ニュースでの引用など、直接話法が好ましい場合は多々あります。一方、インフォーマルあるいはカジュアルな場面で誰かの言葉を正確にそのまま引用することはあまりありません。次の例を見てみましょう。

Eddie: Hey Jon, I'm glad to see you're back. Where have you been?

Jon: Oh, hey Eddie. Well, I went to the countryside with some friends for the weekend, but I got sick and had to stay there a few more days. The weather was terrible there; I couldn't wait to get back.

Eddie: Ooh, that was bad luck! When did you get back?

Jon: Just yesterday, in the evening. How are you doing?

(…数時間後)

Eddie: I talked to Jon today.

Lucy: Oh? What did he say?

Eddie: He said, "I went to the countryside with some friends for the weekend, but I got sick and had to stay there a few more days. The weather was terrible there; I couldn't wait to get back."

Lucy: Oh, so that's why I haven't seen him these days. Did he say when he came back?

Eddie: Yeah, he said, "Just yesterday, in the evening."

エディはルーシーに、ジョンが言ったことを、ジョンが使ったのと全く同じ言葉を使って伝えていることにお気づきでしょうか。文章を書くときには、誰かの言葉を正確に引用する正当な理由があるかもしれません。実生活で、誰かが言ったことを報告するときに、そこまで注意する必要があるのは弁護士とジャーナリストだけでしょう。私たちが直接話法を使って誰かの言葉を引用するとき、話しているときでも書いているときでも、正確な言葉を表現しようとしているかもしれませんが、ほとんどの場合、100％正確ではないことが多く、通常はそれで問題にはなりません。

エディとルーシーの会話を改めて見てみましょう。少し"ズレ"があることにお気づきでしょうか。硬くて、間延びしていて、不自然です。その理由は、エディがジョンの言った言葉を正確にとらえる理由がないからです。言葉の要旨を抽出して伝える方がよほど自然に聞こえることは間違いないでしょう。

2 間接話法（伝聞法）

他者の発言を引用せずに伝える

間接話法では、誰かが言った言葉を正確にとらえようとする努力はしません。むしろ、相手の言葉の「特徴」を伝えます。会話のやりとりの実際的、感情的な「特徴」を捉える努力をするのです。例えば、メアリーと長い会話をした後、その会話をポールに話したり書いたりするなら、メアリーとの会話を要約して伝えます。メアリーが言ったことの中から最も重要な点を選び、それぞれの点に、発話した際の彼女の態度や考え方に合った感情的、状況的な文脈を与える必要があります。ジョンとエディの会話で試してみましょう。

Eddie: Hey Jon, I'm glad to see you back in the office. Where have you been?

Jon: Oh, hey Eddie. Well, I went to the countryside with some friends for the weekend, but I got sick and had to stay there a few more days. The weather was terrible there; I couldn't wait to get back.

Eddie: Ooh, that was bad luck! When did you get back?

Jon: Just yesterday, in the evening. How are you doing?

(…数時間後)

Eddie: I talked to Jon today.

Lucy: Oh? What did he say.

Eddie: He didn't have a very good weekend, I guess. He went to the countryside with some friends, but he got sick and had to stay longer. He said the weather was bad, and he wanted to come back.

Lucy: Oh, so that's why I haven't seen him these days. Did he say when he came back?

Eddie: Yeah, last night.

エディとジョンの会話では、ジョンの週末の過ごし方は、明らかにネガティブなものだったことがわかります。それは悪天候と病気に裏打ちされるわけです。ですから、エディがルー

シーにジョンの言ったことを話したとき、彼はジョンの週末を "not...very good" と表現したのです。

交友関係やビジネスにおいて話す場合でも、他の研究者の学術論文について筆記で言及する場合でも、それをそのまま引用（直接話法）していない場合は、元々聞いたあるいは読んだことばの特徴を伝えることになります。これが間接話法です。

時制の一致

間接話法においては、「時制の一致」というルールが重要です。間接話法の文の最初の動詞が過去であれば、他の直接話法の動詞を一時制ずつ過去にずらして表現します。他の動詞の時制を最初の動詞に一致させます。

直接話法：Alex: I don't know.
間接話法：Alex told me he **didn't know**. （単純現在→単純過去）

直接話法：Alex: I didn't talk to Laura.
間接話法：Alex told me he **hadn't talked to Laura**. （単純過去→過去完了）
※過去完了にすることによって、Alex が私にそれを言った時点より前に発生したことだと明確に伝わります。

直接話法：Alex: I **will** take care of this tomorrow.
間接話法：Alex told me he **would** take care of this the day after. (will → would)
※カジュアルな会話では、時制の一致が厳密には守られない場合も多く見られます。
※間接話法では、時制だけでなく他の時間表現も直接話法とは異なります。Today, yesterday, now といった、直接話法の発話時点を基点とする表現は避け、できるだけ混乱を起こさない表現に変えます。

直接話法	間接話法
yesterday	the day before/ the previous day, on Sunday
today	that day, on Sunday, yesterday
tonight	that night, last night, on Sunday night
tomorrow	the next day/ the following day, on Sunday, today
this week	that week, last week
last night	the night before/ the previous night, on Sunday night
last month	the month before/ the previous month, in May

next year	the following year, in 2014
ten minutes ago	ten minutes before
in an hour	one (an) hour later
now	then, at that time

間接話法の動詞の分類（カジュアルな場面）

間接話法の動詞を分類してみましょう。

まずは、日常会話に使うものと少し硬めのビジネス文章やアカデミック文章で使うものとの分類が可能です。また、書き手や話し手の伝えたいニュアンス次第で、肯定的な意味合いを持つもの、中立的なもの、否定的な意味合いを持つものへの分類もできます。

では、よりカジュアルな場面の間接話法の動詞をみてみましょう。

□ **mention** /ˈmɛnʃən/ **言及する、言う**

○ She mentioned that it might rain tomorrow.

彼女は明日雨が降るかもしれないと言った。

□ **state** /steɪt/ **述べる、言葉にする**

○ He stated that he would be late.

彼は遅くなると述べた。

□ **describe** /dɪˈskraɪb/ **描写する、説明する**

○ They described how the accident happened.

彼らは事故がどのように起こったかを説明した。

□ **note** /noʊt/ **言及する、気づく、言う**

○ He noted that the room was clean.

彼は部屋がきれいだと言った。

inform /ɪnˈfɔːrm/ 知らせる、伝える

○ She informed us that the meeting was cancelled.

彼女は私たちに会議がキャンセルされたと知らせた。

assert /əˈsɜːt/ 主張する、言い張る

○ He asserted his right to speak.

彼は発言する権利を主張した。

declare /dɪˈklɛər/ 宣言する

○ He declared his intentions clearly.

彼は自分の意図をはっきりと宣言した。

suggest /səˈdʒɛst/ 提案する

○ She suggested that we should leave.

彼女は私たちが出発すべきだと提案した。

complain /kəmˈpleɪn/ 不満を言う、苦情を言う、抗議をする

○ They complained about the noise.

彼らは騒音について不満を言った。

remind /rɪˈmaɪnd/ 思い出させる

○ He reminded me about the appointment.

彼は私に予約について思い出させた。

□ **argue** /ˈɑːrgjuː/ **議論する、主張する、立場をとる**

○ She argued that the decision was unfair.
彼女はその決定は不公平だと主張した。

□ **reply** /rɪˈplaɪ/ **答える、返信する**

○ He replied that he didn't know.
彼は知らないと答えた。

□ **answer** /ˈænsər/ **答える、応答する**

○ She answered that she was happy.
彼女は幸せだと答えた。

□ **comment** /ˈkɑːmɛnt/ **コメントする、注釈をつける、論評する**

○ They commented that the food was delicious.
彼らは食事が美味しかったとコメントした。

□ **ask** /æsk/ **尋ねる**

○ He asked if I could help.
彼は私に手伝えるかを尋ねた。

□ **question** /ˈkwɛstʃən/ **疑う、疑問を呈する**

○ She questioned his sincerity.
彼女は彼の誠実さを疑った。

□ **convey** /kənˈveɪ/ 伝える、伝達する、告げる

○ He conveyed his condolences.

彼は哀悼の意を伝えた。

□ **share** /ʃεər/ （情報などを）共有する

○ They shared their plans for the weekend.

彼らは週末の計画を共有した。

□ **admit** /ədˈmɪt/ 認める

○ He admitted that he was wrong.

彼は間違っていたことを認めた。

□ **confirm** /kənˈfɜːm/ 確認する、追認する、発表する

○ She confirmed that she would attend the meeting.

彼女は自分が会議に出席する予定であると伝えた。

□ **reveal** /rɪˈviːl/ 明らかにする

○ He revealed his secret.

彼は自分の秘密を明らかにした。

□ **point out** /ˈpɔɪnt aʊt/ 指摘する

○ She pointed out that the report was incomplete.

彼女は報告書が不完全だと指摘した。

□ **claim** /kleɪm/ **主張する**

○ He claimed that he had been cheated.
彼はだまされたと主張した。

□ **deny** /dɪˈnaɪ/ **否定する**

○ She denied that she was guilty.
彼女は自分が有罪であることを否定した。

□ **promise** /ˈprɑːmɪs/ **約束する**

○ He promised to return the book.
彼は本は返すと約束した。

□ **advise** /ədˈvaɪz/ **助言する**

○ She advised him to study harder.
彼女は彼にもっと一生懸命勉強するように助言した。

□ **insist** /ɪnˈsɪst/ **主張する、断言する**

○ He insisted that he had paid the bill.
彼は自分がその請求を支払ったと主張した。

□ **offer** /ˈɔːfər/ **申し出る、提案する**

○ She offered to help us.
彼女は私たちへの協力を申し出た。

□ **respond** /rɪˈspɑːnd/ 答える、応答する

○ He responded that he was not ready.
彼は準備ができていないと答えた。

□ **acknowledge** /əkˈnɑːlɪdʒ/ 認める

○ She acknowledged her mistake.
彼女は自分の間違いを認めた。

□ **announce** /əˈnaʊns/ 発表する

○ He announced his retirement.
彼は引退を発表した。

□ **report** /rɪˈpɔːrt/ 報告する

○ She reported that the project was a success.
彼女はプロジェクトが成功したと報告した。

□ **disclose** /dɪsˈkloʊz/ 開示する、公表する

○ He disclosed the information to the public.
彼は情報を公に開示した。

□ **express** /ɪkˈsprɛs/ 表する

○ She expressed her gratitude.
彼女は謝意を表した。

□ **agree** /əˈgriː/ 賛成する、同意する

○ They agreed that the plan was well-devised.
彼らはその計画がよく練られていることに同意した。

□ **protest** /ˈproʊˌtɛst/ 抗議する、抵抗する

○ He protested against the decision.
彼は決定に抗議した。

□ **disagree** /ˌdɪsəˈgriː/ 反対する

○ She disagreed with his opinion.
彼の意見に彼女は反対した。

□ **imply** /ɪmˈplaɪ/ 示唆する、ほのめかす、間接的に伝える

○ He implied that something was wrong.
彼は何かが間違っていることを示唆した。

□ **concede** /kənˈsiːd/ 認める、(苦悩の末、しぶしぶ)折れる

○ The author conceded that there might be limitations in the research methodology.
著者は、研究方法論には制約があるかもしれないと認めた。

□ **suggest** /səˈdʒɛst/ 提案する

○ She suggested going to the cinema.
彼女は映画館に行くことを提案した。

□ shout /ʃaʊt/ 叫ぶ、大声で言う

○ He shouted that he was not guilty.

彼は自分が有罪でないと叫んだ。

□ yell /jɛl/ 声を荒げる、叫ぶ

○ She yelled to be careful.

彼女は注意するように叫んだ。

□ murmur /ˈmɝːmər/ つぶやく

○ They murmured about the decision.

彼らは決定についてつぶやいた。

□ mumble /ˈmʌmbəl/ つぶやく

○ He mumbled something about leaving.

彼は出発について何かをつぶやいた。

□ joke /dʒoʊk/ 冗談を言う

○ She joked that she could eat a horse.

彼女は馬一頭だって食べられると冗談を言った。

• (Task 1) •

直接話法を間接話法に書き直してみましょう。

1. "I will be late tonight," said John.

↩ _____

2. "Are you okay?" Mary asked.

↻ _____

3. "I love this restaurant!" exclaimed Sarah.

↻ _____

4. "We need to finish the project by Friday," the manager told the team.

↻ _____

5. "Don't forget to pick up the laundry," Alex reminded Lisa.

↻ _____

6. "I didn't steal the cookies," insisted Tom.

↻ _____

7. "I've finished my homework," Jenny told her mother.

↻ _____

8. "Let's meet at the cinema at 7," proposed Steve.

↻ _____

9. "I can't believe we won the match!" shouted Carlos.

↻ _____

10. "You should get some rest," advised Dr. Brown.

↻ _____

直接話法 (Direct Speech) の文を読んで、間接話法 (Indirect Speech) の文の空所を
埋めるにもっとも適している選択肢を選びましょう。

1. Direct: "The meeting has been postponed," she said.

   Indirect: She _____ that the meeting had been postponed.

   A. answered

   B. reported

   C. complained

   D. joked

2. Direct: "Why don't we go to the park tomorrow?" he said.

   Indirect: He _____ that we should go to the park tomorrow.

   A. admitted

   B. announced

   C. suggested

   D. explained

3. Direct: "I don't think this is fair," she said.

   Indirect: She _____ that she didn't think it was fair.

   A. disclosed

   B. argued

   C. disagreed

   D. agreed

4. Direct: "I've finished the report," he announced.

   Indirect: He _____ that he had finished the report.

   A. shouted

   B. denied

   C. declared

   D. questioned

5. Direct: "The cake was delicious," they said.

Indirect: They _____ that the cake was delicious.

A. commented

B. promised

C. advised

D. retorted

6. Direct: "I swear I will finish the project by tomorrow!" he said.

Indirect: She _____ to finish the project by tomorrow.

A. asked

B. promised

C. expressed

D. murmured

7. Direct: "I am not responsible for the mistake," he said.

Indirect: He _____ being responsible for the mistake.

A. reminded

B. denied

C. stated

D. acknowledged

8. Direct: "It might rain tomorrow," he said.

Indirect: He _____ that it might rain tomorrow.

A. insisted

B. apologized

C. denied

D. mentioned

9. Direct: "Let's meet at 5pm," she suggested.

   Indirect: She _____ meeting at 5pm.

   A. responded

   B. argued

   C. proposed

   D. mumbled

10. Direct: "I can't complete this project alone," he admitted.

   Indirect: He _____ that he couldn't complete the project alone.

   A. denied

   B. conceded

   C. shouted

   D. questioned

Task 3

会話を聞いて、発言の内容をもっとも正しく要約している選択肢を選びましょう。

1. ◀)) u1201

   A. The man told the woman that he didn't like the movie.

   B. The man explained that he had not watched the movie.

   C. The man said he was very impressed.

2. ◀)) u1202

   A. Emily told the teacher that she did not do the homework because it was extremely difficult.

   B. Emily reported to the teacher that she found the homework easy, and was able to finish it.

   C. Emily informed the teacher that she completed the homework despite it being difficult.

3. ◀) u1203

   A. Michael told his boss that the presentation went well, and the clients were receptive of the proposal.

   B. Michael confessed to his boss that the presentation did not go well and the clients disliked their proposals.

   C. Michael reported that the clients were neutral about the proposals.

4. ◀) u1204

   A. The doctor told the patient that his condition was not serious and can be treated.

   B. The doctor admitted to the patient that his condition was serious but assured him it was treatable.

   C. The doctor told the patient that there was no hope for recovery from his condition.

5. ◀) u1205

   A. The Minister told the reporter that he was uncertain about their plans, as these were challenging times.

   B. The Minister confessed that he didn't have any plans for how to handle the crisis.

   C. The Minister assured the reporter that he had a comprehensive plan to handle the crisis.

6. ◀) u1206

   A. Ms. Roberts reported that she had a great time working with him, and that she learned a lot.

   B. Ms. Roberts said she had a terrible experience working with him, but she learned a lot.

   C. Ms. Roberts mentioned that she didn't learn anything from him, but she had a lot of fun.

間接話法 ②

ビジネスや学術研究で文章を書く際、様々な情報源を活用しそれらの有用な情報をまとめて、一貫したオリジナルの文章を作成することが求められます。その際、他の人々が述べたことを報告し、書き手自身の視点を付加して書くことが重要です。最も簡単なレベルでは、間接話法の動詞は単に誰かが何かを述べた（書いた）と伝えるだけです。特定の著者や人物が述べた（書いた）こと、またその人の研究の品質や有用性に対する評価や判断を付加すると、間接話法を使ったもう一段階上の表現が可能になります。間接話法にどの動詞を選択するかは、その評価や判断を正しいニュアンスで伝えられるかを左右します。選択の幅を広げる努力は、書き手としてのパフォーマンスだけでなく、クリティカルシンキングのスキルも向上させます。

1 ─• 間接話法の動詞がもたらすニュアンス

ニュアンス付加で発言の解像度を上げる

質の良い文章を書くためには、どれくらいの間接話法の動詞を語彙力として持つべきでしょうか。明確な答えはありませんが、知っているほど良いと言えます。そういった動詞の使用を学ぶ際の問題の一つは、その数が多いこと、そして多くが非常に似た意味を持つか、わずかに違うだけであるということです。しかし、これらの微妙な違いは、もともとの発言者が言ったこと、著者が公開した論文やジャーナル記事で伝えようとした意図についての重要な情報、つまり意味の強さや含意を伝えることができます。

例えば、多くの場合、say と indicate を差し替えることに大きな違いはないかもしれません。しかし、indicate と suggest を入れ替えると大きな違いが生じます。後者はより

弱く、間接的で、読者や聞き手は著者が実際に書いたことから一つ二つの論理的なステップを踏む必要があり、特定の提案にたどり着く必要があります。

間接話法で伝えている内容に評価的なニュアンスを加えて、その内容の良し悪しや立ち位置に関する付加情報を伝える役割は動詞が果たします。例えば、著者の Brown が Green の研究を学術文献への questionable contribution（疑問視すべき貢献）と書いて、そして学生が論文で Brown suggested (Brown, 2019) that Green's work should not be regarded as useful（Brown によると、Green の論文は有用なものとして見るべきでない）と書いたとします。これは Brown が Green の寄与についてどのように見ているかを正確に伝えることができています。

もう一つの例は、advise と urge の対比に見られます。前者は単に「将来の行動について提案をする」という意味で、後者はより強力な（緊急性のある）、しばしば感情的な誰かの心や行動を変えようとする努力を意味します。間違った動詞を選ぶことは、誰かの意図した意味を誤って伝える可能性があります。

 ② 間接話法の動詞の分類（硬めの場面）

Unit 12 では、カジュアルな場面の間接話法の動詞を扱ってきました。次は、もう少し硬いビジネスやアカデミック文章で役に立つ分類です。伝えたいニュアンス次第で、肯定的、中立的、否定的それぞれの意味合いを持たすことができます。

肯定的なニュアンスを持つ間接話法の動詞

他人の発言に対する同意や肯定を表現する、または他の人の何かに対する同意や承認について報告するには、少し（または強く）肯定的な意味合いを持つ動詞を選びます。これらには以下のようなものが含まれます。

□ applaud /əˈplɔːd/ **拍手する、称賛する**

○ Dr. Livingston applauded the innovative approach the researchers took in their recent study.
リビングストン博士は、研究者たちが最近の研究で取った革新的なアプローチを称賛した。

□ persuade /pərˈsweɪd/ 説得する

○ The CEO successfully persuaded the board members to invest in the new sustainability initiative.

CEOは首尾よく役員たちを新しい持続可能性への取り組みに投資する気にさせることができた。

□ affirm /əˈfɜːrm/ 断言する

○ The researcher confidently affirmed the validity of her data in the academic paper.

研究者は学術論文で自分のデータの妥当性を迷いなく主張した。

□ confirm /kənˈfɜːm/ 確認する

○ The accountant confirmed the accuracy of the financial report released by the company.

会計士はその会社が発表した財務報告の正確さに確信を持った。

□ defend /dɪˈfɛnd/ 防御する

○ The marketing team was able to successfully defend their strategy in the face of criticism.

マーケティングチームは批判の中でもうまく自分たちの戦略を擁護することができた。

□ prove /pruːv/ 証明する

○ She proved her hypothesis by devising a replicable experiment outlined in her new research paper.

彼女は、新しい研究論文に概説されている再現可能な実験を作り上げることで、自分の仮説を証明した。

☐ **favor** /ˈfeɪvər/ **好む**

○ The committee favored the adoption of the new policy.
委員会は新しい政策の採用を支持した。

☐ **contend** /kənˈtɛnd/ **主張する**

○ The manager contended that the new strategy would increase profits and maximize shareholder value.
マネージャーは、新戦略が利益を増加させ、株主利益を最大化させると主張した。

☐ **observe** /əbˈzɜːrv/ **観察する**

○ The analyst observed a significant trend in the market data.
アナリストは市場データで重要なトレンドを観察した。

☐ **support** /səˈpɔːrt/ **支援する**

○ The board supported the proposal for a new project, hoping it would yield the growth the company had been looking for.
役員会は新プロジェクトの提案を支持しており、それは会社が追求してきた成長をもたらすと願ってのことだった。

☐ **encourage** /ɪnˈkʌrɪdʒ/ **奨励する**

○ In order to foster a creative learning environment, the professor encouraged innovative thinking among his students.
創造的な学習環境を育むために、教授は学生間での革新的な思考を奨励した。

☐ **call for** /ˈkɔːl fɔːr/ **要求する**

○ The study called for more attention to environmental factors when considering new construction projects.

その研究は、新規建設工事の検討にあたって環境要素に更なる注目を求めた。

☐ **demonstrate** /ˈdɛmənstreɪt/ **示す**

○ The sales report demonstrated a significant increase in revenue.

営業報告書は、収益の大幅な増加を示した。

☐ **credit** /ˈkrɛdɪt/ **の功績と認める、のお陰である、に帰する**

○ The team credited their success to good leadership.

チームは成功を良いリーダーシップの賜物と評した。

☐ **acknowledge** /əkˈnɑːlɪdʒ/ **認める、認識する**

○ In the introductory part of the book, the author acknowledged the contributions of his colleagues in the research.

書籍の序説部分で、著者は研究における同僚の貢献に謝意を示した（貢献を認めた）。

☐ **agree** /əˈgriː/ **同意する**

○ The board agreed to the proposed changes, qualifying them as progressive and forward-thinking.

進歩的で先見の明のあるものとして、役員会は提案された変更に同意した。

□ **concur** /kənˈkɜː/ **同意する**

○ The academic community concurred with the findings of the research, heralding a new era in the field.

学術界は研究の結果に同意し、その分野に新時代の到来を告げた。

否定的なニュアンスを持つ間接話法の動詞

良い評価を示すのとは逆に、少し（または強く）否定的な意味合いを持つか、または否定的なスタンスを示す動詞には次のようなものがあります。

□ **take issue with** /teɪk ˈɪʃuː wɪð/ **問題にする、問題視する**

○ Smith, in her paper, takes issue with Iverson's conclusion.

スミスは論文でアイバーソンの結論に問題を提起している。

□ **challenge** /ˈtʃæl.ɪndʒ/ **挑戦する、疑問を投げかける**

○ Professor Johnson challenged the prevailing theories on climate change.

ジョンソン教授は気候変動に関する主流の理論に疑問を投げかけた。

□ **call into question** /kɔːl ˈɪntuː ˈkwes.tʃən/ **疑問視する、疑う**

○ The research findings called into question the effectiveness of the new drug.

その研究の結果は、新薬の有効性を疑問視した。

□ **confuse** /kənˈfjuːz/ **混乱させる、困惑させる**

○ The complicated instructions confused the participants in the experiment.
複雑な指示は実験の参加者を混乱させた。

□ **accuse** /əˈkjuːz/ **非難する、告発する**

○ The whistleblower accused the company of financial misconduct.
告発者はその企業を財務不正行為で非難した。

□ **assert** /əˈsɜːrt/ **主張する、断言する**

○ The speaker asserted that the new policy would lead to positive outcomes.
講演者は、新しい方針が良い結果をもたらすと主張した。

□ **doubt** /daʊt/ **疑う、疑問を抱く**

○ The professor doubted the accuracy of the student's research methodology.
教授は学生の研究方法論の正確性を疑問視した。

□ **intimate** /ˈɪn.tɪ.meɪt/ **示唆する、暗示する**

○ The report intimated that there might be a potential conflict of interest.
報告書は潜在的な利益相反があるかもしれないことを示唆した。

□ **allege** /əˈleɪdʒ/ 主張する、申し立てる

○ The article alleged that the company had been involved in illegal practices.

記事は、その企業が違法な活動に関与していたと主張した。

□ **guess** /ges/ 推測する、推量する

○ The researcher guessed that the experiment results were due to a measurement error.

研究者は、実験結果が測定誤差によるものだと推測した。

□ **question** /ˈkwes.tʃən/ 疑問を持つ、問いただす

○ The committee questioned the validity of the data presented in the report.

委員会は、報告書に示されたデータの妥当性を疑問視した。

□ **hope** /hoʊp/ 期待する、望む

○ The researchers hoped that their findings would contribute to the field of neuroscience.

研究者たちは自分たちの研究結果が神経科学の分野に貢献することを望んでいた。

□ **speculate** /ˈspek.jə.leɪt/ 推測する、憶測する

○ The economists speculated that the stock market would experience a downturn.

経済学者たちは、株式市場が下降するだろうと推測した。

□ **refute** /rɪˈfjuːt/ **反論する、論破する**

○ The scientist refuted the claims made by the skeptics with solid evidence.

科学者は、懐疑論者の主張に対し確固たる証拠を基に反論した。

□ **deny** /dɪˈnaɪ/ **否定する、拒絶する**

○ The CEO denied any involvement in the financial scandal.

その CEO はいかなる財務スキャンダルへの関与も否定した。

□ **admit** /ədˈmɪt/ **認める、承認する**

○ The professor admitted that he had made an error in his calculations.

教授は計算に誤りがあったことを認めた。

□ **boast** /boʊst/ **自慢する、誇示する**

○ The company boasted about its record-breaking sales figures at the conference.

その企業は、過去最高を更新した売上高を会議で誇らし気に発表した。

中立的なニュアンスを持つ間接話法の動詞

肯定・否定以外に、中立的な情報伝達を示す動詞も間接話法において重要な一角を担っています。中立的な意味合いを持つ動詞には次のようなものがあります。

□ **address** /əˈdrɛs/ **扱う、話す**

○ Dr. Smith addressed the issue of climate change in his latest paper.

スミス博士は彼の最新の論文で気候変動の問題を取り上げた。

☐ **discuss** /dɪˈskʌs/ **議論する**

○ The committee discussed the implementation of new policies at the meeting.
委員会は会議で新政策の実施について議論した。

☐ **describe** /dɪˈskraɪb/ **描写する**

○ The research paper describes the impact of AI on the job market.
研究論文は、AI が就職市場に与える影響を述べている。

☐ **report** /rɪˈpɔːrt/ **報告する**

○ Johnson et al. (2022) reported a breakthrough in cancer research.
ジョンソンら(2022)は、癌研究の突破口を報告した。

☐ **indicate** /ˈɪndɪkeɪt/ **示す**

○ The data indicate an increase in the rate of inflation.
データはインフレ率の上昇を示している。

☐ **specify** /ˈspɛsɪˌfaɪ/ **明示する**

○ The contract specifies the obligations of both parties.
契約書は両当事者の義務を明示している。

☐ **state** /steɪt/ **述べる**

○ The CEO stated that the company would be investing in renewable energy sources.
CEO は、会社が再生可能エネルギー源に投資すると述べた。

☐ **express** /ɪkˈsprɛs/ 表現する

○ The report expressed concern about the rate of deforestation.
レポートは森林伐採の速度について懸念を表明した。

☐ **propose** /prəˈpoʊz/ 提案する

○ The team proposed a new method for data analysis.
チームはデータ分析の新しい方法を提案した。

☐ **note** /noʊt/ 言及する、注意を払う

○ Brown (2021) noted the lack of resources in rural schools.
ブラウン(2021)は農村の学校の設備不足に言及した。

☐ **suggest** /səˈdʒɛst/ 提案する

○ The study suggests that exercise can improve mental health.
研究は、運動が精神衛生を改善できることを示唆している。

☐ **maintain** /meɪnˈteɪn/ 主張する

○ The author maintains that economic growth does not necessarily lead to happiness.
著者は経済成長が必ずしも幸福につながるわけではないと主張している。

☐ **explain** /ɪkˈspleɪn/ 説明する

○ Professor Lee explained the principles of quantum physics in her lecture.
リー教授は講義で量子物理学の原理を説明した。

□ **add** /æd/ **追加する**

○ In their report, they added that more research was needed.

彼らの報告書には、さらなる研究が必要だと追記されている。

□ **interpret** /ɪnˈtɜːrprɪt/ **解釈する**

○ The analysts interpret the drop in sales as a sign of market saturation.

アナリストたちは売り上げの減少を市場の飽和の兆候と解釈している。

□ **conclude** /kənˈkluːd/ **結論づける**

○ The study concludes that a balanced diet is essential for good health.

研究は、健康維持にはバランスの良い食事が必要であると結論付けている。

□ **wonder** /ˈwʌndər/ **疑問に思う**

○ The researchers wondered about the possible effects of the new drug.

研究者たちはその新薬がもたらし得る効果について疑問を抱いた。

□ **explore** /ɪkˈsplɔːr/ **探求する**

○ The paper explores the correlation between poverty and education.

論文は、貧困と教育との相関関係を詳細に検証している。

間接話法の文を完成させるにもっとも適した動詞を選びましょう。

1.

Quote from Einstein: "The speed of light is independent of the motion of the observer."

Indirect: Einstein, in his special theory of relativity, _____ that the speed of light is independent of the motion of the observer.

    A. doubts

    B. concludes

    C. guesses

    D. explores

2.

Quote from a business analyst: "Despite positive quarterly results, the company may not be able to sustain its growth rate."

Indirect: The business analyst _____ the company's growth sustainability.

    A. applauded

    B. questioned

    C. maintained

    D. defended

3.

Quote from Stephen Hawking: "One can't predict the future."

Indirect: Stephen Hawking _____ the predictability of the future.

    A. applauded

    B. accused

    C. questioned

    D. favored

4.

Quote from an environmental scientist: "We must take immediate action to reduce carbon emissions."

Indirect: The environmental scientist _____ the need for immediate action.

    A. disputed

    B. confirmed

    C. speculated

    D. debunked

5.

Quote from a corporate report: "The company has significantly increased its profits over the last fiscal year."

Indirect: The corporate report _____ the company's increased profits.

    A. defends

    B. alleges

    C. notes

    D. hopes

6.

Quote from Dr. Haller: "The results of the experiment are inconclusive."

Indirect: Dr. Haller _____ the experiment results.

    A. asserts

    B. agrees

    C. contends

    D. takes issue with

7.

Quote from Professor Smith: "The world is experiencing a digital revolution."

Indirect: Professor Smith _____ what he calls "a digital revolution".

    A. confused

    B. observed

    C. asked

    D. refuted

8.

Quote from a book critic: "The book's plot is highly improbable."

Indirect: The book critic _____ the plot of the book.

    A. encourages

    B. recognizes

    C. takes issue with

    D. supports

9.

Quote from a technology expert: "AI is transforming every industry."

Indirect: The technology expert _____ the impact of AI.

    A. downplays

    B. argues

    C. acknowledges

    D. speculates

10.

Quote from an economist: "There's a direct correlation between education and income."

Indirect: The economist _____ a link between education and income.

    A. questions

    B. affirms

    C. wonders

    D. guesses

11.

Quote from a climate scientist: "The warming trend observed over the past few decades is likely due to human activity."

Indirect: The climate scientist _____ that human activity is the cause of the recent warming trend.

    A. doubts

    B. contends

    C. denies

    D. maintains

12.

Quote from a CEO: "Our company is committed to sustainable practices."

Indirect: The CEO _____ the company's commitment to sustainable practices.

    A. boasted

    B. expressed

    C. challenged

    D. speculated

                   (Task 2)

会話を聞いて、設問の答えとしてもっとも適している選択肢を選びましょう。

1. 🔊 u1301

What does John mean?

    A. John accused the attendees of misunderstanding the proposal.

    B. John speculated that the proposal was not well received.

    C. John confirmed that the proposal was poorly received.

    D. John indicated that the proposal was well received.

2. 🔊 u1302

What does Amanda mean?

    A. Amanda applauded the new physics theory.

    B. Amanda called into question the new physics theory.

    C. Amanda agreed with the new physics theory.

    D. Amanda described the new physics theory.

3. 🔊 u1303

What does Claire mean?

    A. Claire challenged the offer made by Thomas.

    B. Claire denied the offer made by Thomas.

    C. Claire stated that she is likely to accept the offer made by Thomas.

    D. Claire expressed confusion about the offer made by Thomas.

4. 🔊 u1304

What does Alex mean?

    A. Alex defended the band's performances.

    B. Alex encouraged going to the concert.

    C. Alex suggested that they shouldn't go to the concert.

    D. Alex doubted if the band was performing this weekend.

5. 🔊 u1305

What does Luke mean?

    A. Luke takes issue with the new lab equipment.

    B. Luke acknowledges that the new lab equipment is great.

    C. Luke hopes the new lab equipment will be better.

    D. Luke describes the new lab equipment as confusing.

6. ◀) u1306

What does Emma mean?

    A. Emma confirmed that the new training was beneficial.

    B. Emma challenged the effectiveness of the new training.

    C. Emma described the new training as intriguing.

    D. Emma boasted about her knowledge from the new training.

7. ◀) u1307

What does Oliver mean?

    A. Oliver accused the art program of being ineffective.

    B. Oliver credited the art program with improving his skills.

    C. Oliver doubted the usefulness of the art program.

    D. Oliver speculated about the effectiveness of the art program.

8. ◀) u1308

What does Lily mean?

    A. Lily called into question the training regimen.

    B. Lily admitted that the training regimen is difficult but beneficial.

    C. Lily denied the usefulness of the training regimen.

    D. Lily hoped the training regimen would be easier.

9. ◀) u1309

What does David mean?

    A. David approves of the new menu at the cafeteria.

    B. David expresses his dislike of the new menu.

    C. David speculates that the new menu might improve.

    D. David contends that the new menu is the best.

10. 🔊 u1310

What does Senator Graham mean?

    A. Senator Graham denies the effectiveness of the new climate policy.

    B. Senator Graham speculates that the new climate policy might work.

    C. Senator Graham supports the new climate policy.

    D. Senator Graham accuses the new climate policy of being misguided.

数字と図表の表現

ビジネスや学術研究といった「真面目な話」をする場面では、数字や図表を使うと、明確かつ正確に意図を伝えることができます。一定のルールを押さえ、ニュアンスを加えてアウトプットの精度を高めることがこの Unit の目的です。

① 数字を図解で伝える

パイチャート

お菓子のパイの形をしていることから「パイチャート」と呼ばれるこのタイプのグラフは、100%で表現できるものの内訳によく使います。ドーナツチャートや三次元パイチャートなどのバリエーションも存在します。

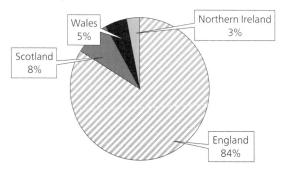

Population distribution of the UK

ここでは、パイチャートを例にグラフの説明でよく使う表現を学びましょう。上記の図の解説の例です。

例

○ The population of the United Kingdom is estimated at 67,081,234 people. As we can see from the chart above, the **overwhelming majority** resides in England. **One in twenty** UK citizens lives in Wales, whereas Northern Ireland, at 3%, has a population **roughly half** that of Wales. While Scotland is the biggest country after England, the Scots are still **a small minority** in the UK, representing 8% of the total population.

イギリスの人口は 67,081,234 人と推定されている。上のグラフからわかるように、**圧倒的多数**がイングランドに住んでいる。イギリス国民の **20 人に 1 人**がウェールズに住み、北アイルランドの人口は 3%で、ウェールズの**およそ半分**である。スコットランドはイングランドに次いで大きな国だが、それでもスコットランド人は**少数派**で、UK 全体の 8%である。

● majority / minority

統計表現として、minority は 49%以内、majority は 51%以上を表しますが、多くのケースでは 2%と 49%をまったく同列には扱うわけにはいきません。そのようなとき、ニュアンスを加えて表現することが重要になります。

1%〜 20%	… a small minority
21%〜 39%	… a minority
40%〜 49%	… a substantial/ significant minority
51%〜 55%	… a small majority
56%〜 79%	… a majority
80%+	… a large majority

overwhelming majority（圧倒的多数）や surprisingly small minority（驚くほどの少数）などの評価的な形容詞や副詞を使うと、あえて発言の中立性の殻を破って自らのスタンスを伝えることができます。

●その他の表現

以下の全てに roughly, approximately, nearly のような副詞を使ってニュアンスを加えることができます。

one in five (ten, four) は実質的にパーセンテージ表現と同じですが、読み手や聞き

手にとって想像しやすいため、よく使われます。英語の感覚として、10% of Chinese people よりも One in ten Chinese といった方が消化しやすいと考えられているわけです。繰り返しを回避するために使われることもあります。

twice as many (seven times as many) は、比較表現です。

○ Twice as many people own a car in Hokkaido as in Tokyo.
北海道では、東京の 2 倍の人々が車を所有しています。

バーチャート（棒グラフ）やラインチャート（折れ線グラフ）

物事の変化・増減・推移を表すのに適しているグラフです。このタイプのグラフを解説する際は、「推移」の描写を念頭においた表現となります。よく使う動詞とそれらにニュアンスを付加するための副詞、また名詞と形容詞の組み合わせを以下にまとめました。存在し得る全てではありませんが、動詞を「上昇」と「下降」の 2 つのカテゴリに分類し、「名詞と形容詞の組み合わせ」としてまとめています。「示す・指す」の意味で、indicate, demonstrate, show などは割愛しています。

上昇、増加を表す動詞

□ rise /raɪz/ 上昇する

○ The line graph shows that prices of commodities rose in the third quarter.
折れ線グラフは、第三四半期に商品の価格が上昇したことを示している。

□ soar /sɔːr/ 急騰する

○ The bar chart indicates that sales soared in December.
棒グラフは 12 月に売上が急騰したことを示している。

☐ **spike** /spaɪk/ 急増する

○ The unemployment rate spiked in January, as the line graph reveals.
折れ線グラフから明らかになっているように、1 月に失業率が急増した。

☐ **climb** /klaɪm/ 登る

○ The bar chart shows that our market share has been steadily climbing.
棒グラフは、私たちの市場シェアが着実に上昇していることを示している。

☐ **increase** /ɪnˈkriːs/ 増加する

○ The number of users has increased over time, as evident from the line graph.
折れ線グラフから明確なように、ユーザー数が時間とともに増加している。

☐ **grow** /ɡrəʊ/ 成長する

○ The bar chart illustrates that the company's revenue has been growing.
棒グラフは、会社の収入が成長していることを示している。

☐ **surge** /sɜːrdʒ/ 急上昇する

○ The line graph depicts the extent to which demand for our product has surged.
折れ線グラフは、当社製品に対する需要がいかに急上昇したかを描いている。

☐ **jump** /dʒʌmp/ 飛び上がる

○ Sales figures jumped in the last quarter, as evident from the bar chart.
棒グラフは、最後の四半期に売上数字が大幅に跳ね上がったことを示している。

□ **escalate** /ˈeskəˌleɪt/ **次第に上昇する**

○ The line graph indicates that the cost of raw materials has been escalating.

折れ線グラフは、原材料のコストが次第に上昇していることを示している。

□ **advance** /ədˈvæns/ **進む**

○ The line graph demonstrates how the project has advanced since January.

折れ線グラフは、プロジェクトが 1 月以来どう進んでいるかを示している。

□ **amplify** /ˈæmplɪˌfaɪ/ **増幅する**

○ The bar chart shows that our efforts have helped to amplify the brand's reach.

棒グラフは、当社の努力がブランドのリーチを増幅させるのに役立っていることを示している。

□ **expand** /ɪkˈspænd/ **拡大する**

○ The line graph exhibits how the customer base has expanded over the years.

折れ線グラフは、顧客基盤が何年にもわたって拡大してきたことを示している。

□ **strengthen** /ˈstreŋkθən/ **強化する**

○ The bar chart reflects the steps taken to strengthen our market position.

棒グラフは、マーケットポジションを強化するための取り組みを反映している。

□ **mount** /maʊnt/ **増す**

○ The line graph shows mounting pressures on our supply chain due to increased demand.

折れ線グラフは、需要の増加により供給チェーンに対する圧力が増していることを示している。

□ **multiply** /ˈmʌltɪˌplaɪ/ **増やす**

○ The line graph shows how our investments have multiplied over the years.

折れ線グラフは、当社の投資が何年にもわたって増えてきたことを示している。

□ **improve** /ɪmˈpruːv/ **改善する**

○ The line graph demonstrates how the company's performance has improved.

折れ線グラフは、会社のパフォーマンスがどのように改善したかを示している。

□ **ascend** /əˈsɛnd/ **上昇する**

○ The bar chart indicates the ascending trend of our sales figures.

棒グラフは、売上金額の上昇傾向を示している。

□ **shoot up** /ʃuːt ʌp/ **急騰する**

○ The line graph shows how the company's stock prices shot up after the announcement.

折れ線グラフは、発表後に会社の株価が急騰したことを示している。

下降、下落を表す動詞

□ **fall** /fɔːl/ **落ちる**

○ The bar chart shows how the company's profit margins fell during the pandemic.

棒グラフは、パンデミック期間中に会社の利益率がいかに落ちたかを示している。

□ **drop** /drɑːp/ **下がる**

○ Sales dropped significantly during the first quarter, as illustrated by the line graph.

第一四半期に売上が大幅に下がったことが、折れ線グラフに示されている。

□ **decline** /dɪˈklaɪn/ **減少する**

○ As you can see from the bar chart, customer satisfaction has declined since the last survey.

棒グラフを見てわかるように、前回のアンケートより顧客満足度が低下している。

□ **decrease** /dɪˈkriːs/ **減少する**

○ Our annual revenue decreased owing to the lockdowns in Europe, as the line graph indicates.

折れ線グラフが示すように、当社の年商は欧州のロックダウン期間中に減少した。

□ **shrink** /ʃrɪŋk/ **縮小する**

○ The bar chart shows how our market share has shrunk over the years.

棒グラフは、当社の市場シェアが何年にもわたって縮小してきたことを示している。

☐ **diminish** /dɪˈmɪnɪʃ/ **減少する**

○ The line graph depicts the diminishing returns on our investments.
折れ線グラフは、投資の収益が減少していることを示している。

☐ **dwindle** /ˈdwɪndl/ **縮小する**

○ The bar chart indicates how interest in our product has dwindled.
棒グラフは、当社の製品への関心が縮小したことを示している。

☐ **sink** /sɪŋk/ **沈む**

○ The line graph shows a sinking trend in our market presence.
折れ線グラフは、当社の市場存在感が沈みつつある傾向を示している。

☐ **dive** /daɪv/ **急落する**

○ The bar chart displays a dive in stock prices after the negative news.
棒グラフは、悪いニュースの後に株価が急落したことを示している。

☐ **plunge** /plʌndʒ/ **急落する**

○ As evident from the bar chart, the company's net profit has plunged since we hired 30 new engineers.
棒グラフから明らかなように、会社の純利益は 30 名のエンジニアを新たに雇用して以降急落した。

☐ **tumble** /ˈtʌmbl/ **転倒する**

○ The line graph demonstrates how production rates have tumbled.
折れ線グラフは、いかに生産率が転倒したかを示している。

□ **lower** /ˈloʊər/ **下げる**

○ The bar chart indicates the company's efforts to lower operating costs.
棒グラフは、会社の運用コスト削減に向けた努力を示している。

□ **double** /ˈdʌbl/ **倍増する**

○ Figure 1 indicates that after the merger, our customer base nearly doubled.
合併後、当社の顧客基盤はほぼ倍増したことが図の1で示されている。

□ **halve** /hæv/ **半減する**

○ The bar chart demonstrates that supply chain issues were the reason why our company had to halve its production.
サプライチェーンの問題により、会社は生産量を半減せざるを得なかったことがこの棒グラフで示されている。

□ **lessen** /ˈlɛsən/ **減らす**

○ The line graph shows the effect of initiatives taken to lessen the impact on the environment.
折れ線グラフは、環境への影響を減らすための取り組みの効果を示している。

□ **contract** /kənˈtrækt/ **縮小する**

○ The bar chart demonstrates that the consumer market has contracted significantly.
棒グラフは、消費者市場が顕著に縮小していることを示している。

□ **ebb** /εb/ **減退する**

○ The line graph depicts how customer demand ebbs during the off-season.

折れ線グラフは、オフシーズン中の顧客の需要がいかに減退するかを示している。

□ **weaken** /ˈwiːkən/ **弱くする**

○ The line graph clearly shows that our company's performance has weakened.

折れ線グラフは、当社のパフォーマンスが弱まっていることを明示している。

□ **subside** /səbˈsaɪd/ **減退する**

○ The bar chart indicates that the initial surge in sales has subsided.

棒グラフは、当初の販売急増にブレーキがかかったことを示している。

上昇、増加の表現 ―― 名詞と形容詞の組み合わせ

□ **sharp rise　急激な上昇**

○ The line graph shows a sharp rise in the company's profits in the second quarter.

折れ線グラフは、第二四半期に企業の利益が急激に上昇したことを示している。

□ **steady increase　安定した増加**

○ There has been a steady increase in our customer base over the past year.

過去 1 年間にわたり、当社の顧客基盤は安定した増加を示している。

□ sudden jump　突然の飛躍

○ There was a sudden jump in sales after the holiday campaign.
ホリデーキャンペーン後に売上が突然飛躍的に増加した。

□ gradual climb　徐々の上昇

○ The bar chart represents a gradual climb in revenue over the last three months.
棒グラフは、過去 3 ヶ月間で収益が徐々に上昇したことを示している。

□ massive surge　大幅な急騰

○ We saw a massive surge in website traffic after the product launch.
商品の発売後、ウェブサイトのトラフィックが爆発的に増加した。

□ substantial growth　かなりの成長

○ The company has experienced substantial growth in market share this year.
会社は今年、市場シェアにおいてかなりの成長を経験した。

□ significant advance　重要な進展

○ There has been a significant advance in the company's performance this quarter.
会社の今年の四半期の業績は重要な進展を遂げている。

□ **slight improvement　わずかな改善**

○ We noticed a slight improvement in customer satisfaction ratings this month.
今月、顧客満足度の評価がわずかに改善した。

□ **notable expansion　注目すべき拡大**

○ The line graph shows a notable expansion in our global market reach.
折れ線グラフは、当社のグローバルマーケットへの浸透の注目すべき拡大を示している。

□ **remarkable ascent　顕著な上昇**

○ The bar chart indicates a remarkable ascent in software downloads last week.
棒グラフは、先週のソフトウェアダウンロードが顕著に上昇したことを示している。

□ **steep shoot up　急激な上昇**

○ We noticed a steep shoot up in online sales during the holiday season.
ホリデーシーズン中にオンラインセールスが急激に上昇した。

減少、降下の表現 ── 名詞と形容詞の組み合わせ

□ **drastic fall　劇的な落ち込み**

○ The graph shows a drastic fall in company stocks after the negative news.
グラフは、ネガティブなニュースの後に企業の株式が劇的に落ち込んだことを示している。

□ **minimal drop　最小限の落ち込み**

○ We observed a minimal drop in user engagement last month.
先月、ユーザーエンゲージメントは最小限の落ち込みにとどまった。

□ **significant decline　著しい減少**

○ The chart illustrates a significant decline in the company's net profit.
チャートは、会社の純利益の著しい減少を示している。

□ **major decrease　大きな減少**

○ The company saw a major decrease in sales in the first quarter.
会社は、第一四半期に売上の大きな減少を見た。

□ **minor shrinkage　わずかな縮小**

○ The bar chart indicates a minor shrinkage in the market size.
棒グラフは市場規模がわずかに縮小したことを示している。

□ **gradual diminishment　段階的な減少**

○ We witnessed a gradual diminishment in the customer retention rate.
顧客維持率が徐々に低下している。

□ **severe plunge　深刻な急落**

○ The company's stock took a severe plunge following the scandal.
スキャンダル後、会社の株価は深刻な急落を見せた。

□ **gentle slump　緩やかなスランプ**

○ There has been a gentle slump in the company's revenue over the past two months.

過去 2 ヶ月間で、会社の収入は緩やかなスランプを見せている。

□ **dramatic tumble　劇的な急落**

○ The company's stock experienced a dramatic tumble after the announcement.

発表後、会社の株価は劇的な急落を経験した。

□ **small reduction　小さな減少**

○ The graph shows a small reduction in operating costs this month.

グラフは、今月の運用費がやや減少したことを示している。

□ **marked contraction　顕著な収縮**

○ The company has experienced a marked contraction in its domestic market.

会社は、国内市場で顕著な収縮を経験した。

□ **massive slide　大幅な下落**

○ After the failed product launch, the company experienced a massive slide in its stock prices.

新商品投入に失敗した後、会社の株価は大幅に下落した。

□ slight weakening　わずかな弱化

○ The graph indicates a slight weakening in demand for our product.
グラフは、当社の製品への需要がわずかに弱まっていることを示している。

□ rapid dive　急速な落ち込み

○ The graph depicts a rapid dive in the company's share price after the quarterly results were announced.
四半期決算の発表後、会社の株価は急速に落ち込んだ。

□ sudden descent　突然の下降

○ The company experienced a sudden descent in stock prices after the CEO's resignation.
CEO の辞任後、会社の株価は突然下降した。

□ significant dwindling　著しい減少

○ The company has seen a significant dwindling in its market position this year.
今年、会社の市場における地位は著しい後退を見せている。

以下でグラフを用いた説明の一例を見てみましょう。

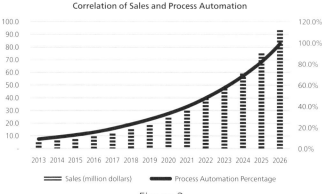

Figure 2

例

○ We started introducing process automation to our manufacturing process in 2010, and our adoption rate was just below 10% in 2013. Since then, we have been gradually increasing automation, and in 2026 all of our processes will have an element of automation introduced. Figure 2 indicates how our sales figures have gone up over this period, tightly correlated with the introduction of process automation.

当社は 2010 年に製造工程へのプロセス自動化の導入を開始しましたが、導入率は 2013 年にはわずかに 10%未満でした。それ以来、自動化を徐々に増加させてきており、2026 年にはすべてのプロセスに自動化の要素が導入される予定です。

図 2 はこの期間にわたって売上数値がどのように上昇してきたかを示し、プロセス自動化の導入と密接に関連していることが読み取れます。

●その他の図表

demonstrate, indicate, show, reveal などの動詞を使って描写します。他のタイプの図表に関しても言えることですが、書いてある数字を文字通りに繰り返すのではなく、図表を見せながら、内容を概念化して伝えることが良いとされます。例えば、何かが 25%から 75%に増えたとすれば、XX was 25% but now is 75% のような言い方よりも、XX tripled over the period / XX significantly increased のように図表が語っているエッセンスを伝えることが重要です。

Table 表

項目が多くて、パイチャートや棒グラフに適さない内容であれば表を選びましょう。内容を表現するにはパイチャートや棒グラフなどと同じ語彙が使えます。

Org chart (organizational chart) 組織図における語彙

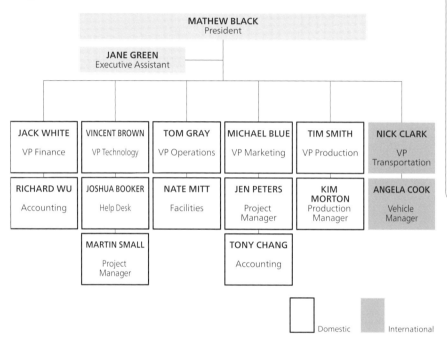

□ **hierarchy** /ˈhaɪəˌrɑrki/ **階層**

○ This organization chart shows a clear hierarchy with the CEO at the top.

この組織図は、CEO がトップにいる明確な階層を示している。

☐ **node** /noʊd/ ノード

○ In this org chart, each node represents a different department within the company.

この組織図では、各ノードが会社内の異なる部門を表している。

☐ **subordinate** /sə'bɔːrdɪnət/ **部下**

○ According to the org chart, the marketing manager is a subordinate of the Director of Operations.

組織図によれば、マーケティングマネージャーは業務部長の部下である。

☐ **superior** /suː'pɪəriər/ **上司**

○ In the org chart, the Chief Financial Officer (CFO) is the superior of the Finance Department.

組織図では、最高財務責任者(CFO)は財務部門の上司である。

☐ **chain of command** /tʃeɪn əv kə'mɑːnd/ **指揮系統**

○ The chain of command in this org chart flows from the CEO to the interns.

この組織図の指揮系統は CEO からインターンにまで及んでいる。

☐ **span of control** /spæn əv kən'troʊl/ **管理範囲**

○ This middle manager's span of control seems to be 5 subordinates.

この中間管理職の管理範囲は 5 人の部下であるようだ。

□ **matrix structure** /ˈmeɪtrɪks ˈstrʌktʃər/ **マトリックス構造**

○ Our organization follows a matrix structure, as evident from the multiple reporting lines in the org chart.

我々の組織は、組織図の複数の報告ラインから明らかなように、マトリックス構造をとっている。

□ **functional structure** /ˈfʌŋkʃənl ˈstrʌktʃər/ **機能的構造**

○ Our org chart is based on a functional structure where each department specializes in a specific function.

我々の組織図は、各部門が特定の機能を専門とする機能構造に基づいている。

□ **divisional structure** /dɪˈvɪʒənl ˈstrʌktʃər/ **部門構造**

○ As you can see from our org chart, we follow a divisional structure, grouping employees based on product lines.

我々の組織図からわかるように、当社は製品ラインに基づいて従業員をグループ化する部門構造を採用している。

□ **flat structure** /flæt ˈstrʌktʃər/ **フラット構造**

○ The org chart shows a flat structure with very few management levels between the CEO and the workers.

組織図は、CEO と作業員の間に管理レベルがほとんどないフラット構造を示している。

□ **tall structure** /tɔːl ˈstrʌktʃər/ **高層階層構造**

○ Our org chart represents a tall structure, with many levels of management from top to bottom.

我々の組織図は、上から下まで多くの管理レベルを持つ高い階層構造を表している。

□ vertical linkage /ˈvɜːrtɪkl ˈlɪŋkɪdʒ/ 垂直連結

○ The vertical linkage between the Marketing Head and his subordinates is clearly shown in the chart.

マーケティングヘッドとその部下との間の垂直連結は、チャートで明確に示されている。

□ horizontal linkage /hɔːrɪˈzɒntl ˈlɪŋkɪdʒ/ 水平連結

○ In the org chart, the horizontal linkage between different departments can be observed.

組織図では、異なる部門間の水平連結が観察できる。

□ centralization /ˌsɛntrəlɪˈzeɪʃən/ 集中化

○ The org chart reveals a high degree of centralization, with major decisions made at the top level.

組織図は、主要な決定がトップレベルで行なわれるという高度な集中化を明らかにしている。

□ decentralization /diːˌsɛntrəlɪˈzeɪʃən/ 分権化

○ Looking at our org chart, you can see a fair amount of decentralization, with decision-making authority at various levels.

当社の組織図を見ると、決定権が様々なレベルにあることから、相当な分権化が見て取れる。

□ organizational layers /ˌɔːrgənɪˈzeɪʃənl ˈleɪərz/ 組織階層

○ This org chart shows the various organizational layers, from the executives to the front-line employees.

この組織図は、エグゼクティブからフロントラインの従業員までのさまざまな組織階層を示している。

2 → 数字を用いない数量的表現

図表を語る場面で、様々な数量的表現も使います。一般的な数字やパーセンテージに加え、数字を用いない数量的表現もアウトプットのレパートリーに備えておくことでより幅広い表現力が生まれます。

「いくつかの」―few, a few, several

few「期待値や予想値より少ない」という意味ですが、a few は「少量の、いくつか」といった意味です。a few は中立的な語彙で、期待値を前提としていません。several は a few に非常に似ていますが、人によっては a few より少し多い時に使います。

○ Few people were interested in the excursion.

　　旅行に興味を示した人はあまりいませんでした。

○ A few people were interested in the excursion.

　　何人かは旅行に興味を示しました。

○ I'll talk to my lawyer and will get back to you in several days.

　　弁護士と相談して、数日後にご連絡します。

「多くの」―dozens of, scores of, hundreds of, thousands of

dozen /ˈdʌzn/ は元々 12 の塊を指しますが、dozens と複数形で使うと、大雑把には 30 ～ 60 を指し、「けっこう多い」という意味合いです。多いが、数えきれないほどではない数量を示すので、そのニュアンスを意識しましょう。これは、昔の英国が 12 進法で数えていた時代の名残りです。scores /skɔːrs/ (複数) 単数では、20 を示しますが、複数で使うと「数えられるたくさん」を意味します。通常は 60 ～ 100 程度でしょう。

例

○ The company has received dozens of applications for the new position.
会社は新しい職位に対して数十の応募を受け取りました。

○ The new product has attracted scores of interested customers.
新製品は多くの(=数十人の)顧客を引きつけました。

hundred や thousand を複数で使うと、数百や数千という意味合いで「たくさん」を示します。

例

○ The marketing campaign reached hundreds of potential clients.
マーケティングキャンペーンは数百人の潜在的なクライアントに到達しました。

○ Our website gets thousands of visitors each day.
私たちのウェブサイトは毎日数千人の訪問者を獲得します。

many や a lot of の代わりに使える「たくさんの」
— a plethora of, a slew of, an array of

a plethora /'pleθ ərə/ of, a slew /slu:/ of, an array /ə'reɪ/ of は、すべて「たくさん」という意味です。a lot や many のやや複雑な言い方や強調表現だと思って使ってください。微細な違いですが、plethora と slew は「過剰なほど多い」や「多くて圧倒される」のニュアンスでも使えますが、array はこのニュアンスで使えません。一方、array は「幅広い、多彩な」といったニュアンスがあります。

例

○ The manager has a plethora of tasks to complete before the deadline.
マネージャーは期限前に完了するべき多数のタスクを持っています。

○ The HR department received a slew of applications for the internship position.
人事部はインターンシップのポジションにたくさんの応募を受け取りました。

○ The accounting department uses an array of software tools for financial analysis.

会計部は財務分析のためのさまざまなソフトウェアツールを使用します。

much と many は一般的に、可算名詞なら many、不可算名詞なら much というように使い分けます。これは、別の言い方をすると、many は「数」、much は「度合」とも言えます。

○ Many employees went home early that day.

その日は、多くの社員が早退しました。

○ The flavor of this tea is much stronger than the one we had yesterday.

このお茶は、昨日よりずいぶん味が濃いようです。

1 つ目の文は、数えようと思えば正確な数が調べられるといった含みがあります。
2 つ目の文は、定量評価が難しい(数えられない)もので、度合を表現しています。

Jack, Lucy, Alex の 3 人の会話を聞いて、どの人がどのグラフに言及しているかを選択しましょう。それぞれの発言者に関して ① ② ③ ④ のいずれかに丸を書いてください。

🔊 u1401

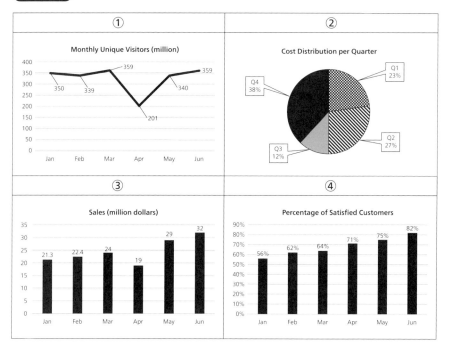

Question: Which visual is each of the speakers referring to?

Jack : ① ② ③ ④

Lucy : ① ② ③ ④

Alex : ① ② ③ ④

○━━━━━━━━━━•(Task 2)•━━━━━━━━━━○

ある商業施設の担当者が以下の図表を見せながら社内プレゼンテーションをしています。プレゼンテーションのスクリプトの空所に入る最も適切な選択肢をそれぞれから選びましょう。

◀)) u1402

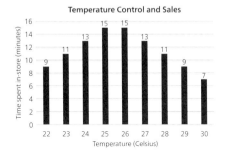

Temperature Control and Sales

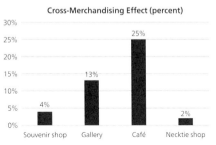

Cross-Merchandising Effect (percent)

In addition to the issues we discussed, there are two more items I'd like to draw your attention to. First, [1]_____ . During the hot months, we tend to believe that the cooler we make the place, the longer people will hang out, and [2]_____ , the more they'll buy from the various shops on each floor. However, that's not always the case. The data we took clearly [3]_____ that if it is too hot, customers spend only the minimum amount of time in-store. As counter-intuitive as it may be, the same data demonstrates that [4]_____ the temperature too much during the hot months drives customers away just as much. 25-26 degrees is apparently the [5]_____ summer temperature. At 22 degrees, there is a [6]_____ in the time they spend with us. Similarly, at 30 degrees it [7]_____ .

Another item on the agenda is what kind of tenant we should look for to fill in the vacancy on the 4th floor. I found some data from other department stores, and based on these data, I believe we should rethink our original idea to rent the space to a gallery. The data represents the [8]_____ of customers who came to visit one specific store but also ended up making unplanned purchases from other stores. Needless to say, we want the customers to purchase from multiple stores. In that respect, renting to a café is by far the best option, in my opinion. If we have a café on the 4th floor we can practically [9]_____ the cross-merchandising effect.

(1) A. customer acquisition   B. cost control
    C. temperature control   D. control

(2) A. therefore   B. nevertheless
    C. regardless   D. unfortunately

(3) A. negates   B. indicates   C. decreases   D. opposes

(4) A. increasing   B. augmenting   C. attempting   D. lowering

(5) A. optimal   B. worst   C. unknown   D. defiant

(6) A. steep climb   B. sharp decline   C. major increase   D. no change

(7) A. goes up significantly   B. declines by more than half
    C. becomes optional   D. nearly triples

(8) A. minority   B. majority   C. face   D. percentage

(9) A. double   B. halve   C. quadruple   D. slash

総仕上げ問題

この Unit では、ここまでの内容を総復習するための問題を用意しました。解いてみてあまり自信を持てなかった場合、あるいはセルフチェックしてみたら間違いが多かった場合は、それぞれの Unit をもう一度読み、感覚を掴んでから再挑戦するとより効果的です。

 Unit 1～3

空所を埋めるための適切な語句を選びましょう

1. _____ the heavy rain, the school event has been postponed.
   A. Owing to
   B. To benefit
   C. To disadvantage
   D. To merit

2. One of the _____ of online learning is the flexibility it offers.
   A. drawbacks
   B. benefits
   C. because of
   D. causes

3. Smoking _____ numerous health problems, including heart disease.
   A. is caused by
   B. leads to
   C. plus
   D. negatively effects

4. The recent policy change can be _____ the efforts of the community activists.
   A. attributed to
   B. advantaged by
   C. seen as the downside of
   D. for

5. One _____ of living in the city is the easy access to public transportation.
   A. demerit
   B. because
   C. cause
   D. merit

6. The rise in temperatures _____ an increase in forest fires in the region.
   A. was caused by
   B. is an advantage for
   C. merits
   D. is beneficial for

7. The _____ of this strategy is that it may alienate some long-term customers.
   A. reason
   B. cause
   C. disadvantage
   D. attribution

8. The new feature has been welcomed by users _____ its user-friendliness.
   A. thanks to
   B. since
   C. because
   D. caused by

9. _____ rigorous training, the team was able to achieve a resounding victory.
   A. Leading to
   B. Negatively influenced by
   C. Owing to
   D. Disadvantaged by

10. The _____ of using renewable energy sources is that they can reduce the carbon footprint significantly.
    A. negative aspect
    B. positive effect
    C. main reason
    D. disadvantage

11. Increased water pollution _____ the dumping of industrial waste in the river.
    A. multiple upsides
    B. advantages are
    C. has drawbacks
    D. can be attributed to

12. Insufficient rainfall will _____ a significant decrease in crop yields, affecting the livelihoods of many farmers.

A. downside

B. disadvantage

C. produce

D. due to

13. The decision to work remotely has its _____ , such as decreased commuting time, and fewer opportunities for communication with coworkers.

A. advantages

B. results in

C. pros and cons

D. since

14. _____ the lack of evidence, the theory cannot be accepted as true.

A. Benefiting

B. Due to

C. One positive aspect of

D. Producing

15. The _____ of this material is its high resistance to heat and chemicals.

A. advantage

B. main cause

C. pros and cons

D. reason

B • Unit 4

空所を埋めるための適切な語句を選びましょう

1. Until 1962, St Paul's Cathedral had been _____ building for over 250 years.
   A. London's the tallest
   B. London's tallest
   C. taller than London
   D. as tall as London

2. If I were _____ my brother, I would be a wrestler too.
   A. strongest
   B. the strongest
   C. more strong
   D. as strong as

3. The United States is _____ than Germany.
   A. largest
   B. the larger
   C. significantly larger
   D. half as large

4. The likelihood of experiencing snow is _____ if you go there in January.
   A. as high as
   B. much higher
   C. most high
   D. most highest

5. Having _____ is important if you want to succeed in business.

A. a narrower focus

B. as narrow a focus as

C. most narrow focus

D. the narrowest of focuses

6. Everyone thought that Jane had the _____ argument.

A. deeper

B. higher

C. stronger

D. more

7. This book helped me gain a _____ understanding of epistemology.

A. higher

B. higher

C. more

D. deeper

8. Gamers typically look for _____ computers and bigger monitors.

A. more fast

B. faster

C. fastest

D. as fast as

9. To become an Olympic champion, you need to run at least _____ than the second guy.

A. as fast

B. much faster

C. slightly faster

D. fastest

10. My _____ friend Brian is getting married on Saturday.
    A. the best
    B. best
    C. better
    D. the better

C — Unit 5〜6

1. 下記の文の空所に if か when を入れて完成させましょう。

1. _____ you decide to come to the party, please let me know.

2. I will call you _____ I arrive at the airport.

3. She will be very happy _____ she receives your gift.

4. _____ it rains tomorrow, we will have to cancel the picnic.

5. They will announce their decision _____ the meeting concludes.

6. _____ you you're next in Tokyo, don't forget to try the sushi at the Tsukiji market.

7. _____ we don't receive the shipment by Friday, we will contact the supplier.

8. I will send you the report _____ I finish it.

9. _____ you fail the exam, ask the teacher for help.

10. We will go for a hike _____ the weather is nice this weekend.

2. 空所を埋める正しい選択肢を選びましょう。

1. He would be an expert in Japanese _____ he practiced daily for years.
   A. when
   B. if
   C. while
   D. since

2. She would have succeeded if she _____ harder.
   A. works
   B. worked
   C. had worked
   D. working

3. I would be happier if he _____ more often.
   A. visits
   B. visited
   C. will visit
   D. had visited

4. If it _____ tomorrow, we will have a picnic.
   A. don't rain
   B. didn't rain
   C. doesn't rain
   D. won't rain

5. They would be here by now _____ they had caught the early train.
   A. since
   B. if
   C. when
   D. although

6. She wishes she _____ the piano as a child.
   A. learns
   B. learned
   C. had learned
   D. will learn

7. If you _____ the truth, I will forgive you.
   A. tells
   B. told
   C. tell
   D. will tell

8. They could have visited the museum if they _____ earlier.
   A. arrives
   B. arrived
   C. will arrive
   D. had arrived

9. She would have felt better _____ she had taken her medicine.
   A. although
   B. if
   C. while
   D. since

10. You would have known the answer _____ you paid attention in class.
    A. when
    B. has
    C. had
    D. having

11. I will lend you the money, _____ you pay me back by the end of the month.

    A. although

    B. provided

    C. when

    D. while

12. If she _____ to the concert, she would have met the singer.

    A. goes

    B. went

    C. had gone

    D. was going

13. I wish I _____ more time to spend with my family.

    A. has

    B. have

    C. had

    D. having

14. He will finish the project on time if he _____ now.

    A. starts

    B. will start

    C. had started

    D. starting

15. I wish I _____ her when I had the chance.

    A. has told

    B. will tell

    C. told

    D. had told

Unit 8

1. We visited several museums in the city, _____ the Natural History Museum and the art gallery.
   A. for example
   B. yet another
   C. on top of that
   D. to put it another way

2. I believe the project will be a success; _____ , it has the backing of several prominent industry leaders.
   A. including
   B. moreover
   C. regardless
   D. another aspect

3. The scientist made a significant discovery; _____ , he found a way to improve the efficiency of solar panels by 20%.
   A. nevertheless
   B. furthermore
   C. notwithstanding
   D. namely

4. The trip was not only educational but _____ fun and exciting.
   A. also
   B. in other words
   C. including
   D. namely

5. This Japanese company has been rapidly expanding throughout Asia. _____ , the company plans to expand its operations to European markets in the coming years.

A. To put it simply

B. Furthermore

C. Like

D. One more

6. The documentary was extremely informative; it covered various topics, _____ climate change and conservation efforts.

A. such as

B. to sum up

C. by the way

D. on top of that

7. The artist's performance at the concert was incredible. _____ , the lighting and sound system were top-notch.

A. In other words

B. Furthermore

C. To illustrate

D. Including

8. He is a talented musician, playing instruments _____ guitar, piano, and drums.

A. in a nutshell

B. such as

C. to put it simply

D. to sum up

9. She helped organize the potluck, brought games for everyone, and played the piano. _____ , she also brought a homemade apple pie.
   A. for example
   B. yet another
   C. particularly
   D. in addition

10. The book covers a lot of complex theories; _____ , it includes a section on quantum physics.
    A. on top of that
    B. to put it another way
    C. by the way
    D. that is to say

11. The new mall has a wide range of stores, _____ a cinema and a large food court.
    A. on top of that
    B. including
    C. therefore
    D. in other words

12. The report outlined several potential solutions, _____ increasing funding for public transportation.
    A. another aspect
    B. namely
    C. including
    D. one more

13. I know you want to see it, so I won't reveal much. _____ , the movie was both thrilling and thought-provoking.

   A. In a nutshell

   B. In particular

   C. For instance

   D. One more

14. I have visited several countries in Europe, _____ France, Italy, and Germany.

   A. moreover

   B. yet another

   C. such as

   D. another aspect

15. The artist is known for his unique style; _____ , his paintings often feature vibrant colors and abstract shapes.

   A. On the contrary

   B. Namely

   C. Regardless

   D. Additionally

16. The show was excellent. _____ , the lead actor delivered a phenomenal performance.

   A. In particular

   B. To sum up

   C. By the way

   D. Like

17. The novel had a very interesting plot; _____ , it gave deep insights into the human psyche.

    A. by the way

    B. therefore

    C. for instance

    D. furthermore

18. He is an expert in many areas of science, _____ physics and chemistry.

    A. including

    B. to illustrate

    C. by the way

    D. one more

19. They decided to renovate the entire house; _____ , they plan to add a new garden.

    A. another aspect

    B. one more

    C. in addition

    D. such as

20. The technology is innovative and, _____ , it has the potential to revolutionize the whole industry.

    A. in other words

    B. what's more

    C. for example

    D. another aspect

文を完成させるにもっとも適した語句を選びましょう。

1. He had a minor accident in the morning; _____ , he managed to arrive at the meeting on time.
   A. in spite of
   B. instead of
   C. whereas
   D. nevertheless

2. She is very good at playing the piano; _____ , she cannot play the violin.
   A. however
   B. instead of
   C. regardless
   D. notwithstanding

3. The Northern region experiences cold and snowy winters, _____ , the Southern region enjoys warm and sunny weather.
   A. in contrast
   B. instead
   C. despite
   D. nevertheless

4. She had all the qualifications for the job; _____ , she wasn't selected.
   A. still
   B. instead of
   C. whereas
   D. instead

5. He is known for his calm demeanor, _____ his sister is quite impulsive.

    A. on the contrary

    B. thus

    C. whereas

    D. despite

6. Many people recommended the movie, _____ I didn't enjoy it very much.

    A. notwithstanding

    B. yet

    C. instead

    D. despite

7. He still makes time to mentor new employees, _____ he has a very important role in the company.

    A. even though

    B. instead

    C. conversely

    D. on the contrary

8. _____ the rain, they decided to go ahead with the picnic.

    A. Regardless of

    B. Instead

    C. Conversely

    D. On the contrary

9. He doesn't like sweets; _____ he ate the piece of cake so as not to offend the host.

    A. notwithstanding

    B. instead of

    C. whereas

    D. nevertheless

10. She doesn't enjoy going to the gym, _____ she goes there every day to maintain her health.

   A. in contrast

   B. although

   C. instead

   D. conversely

表を埋めるための英語語義を作ってみましょう。一行目は例として掲載しています。

word	category	application/location/details
a pencil	*is a tool*	*used for writing*
a bicycle		
a bakery		
a balcony		
a battery		
a brochure		
a cafeteria		
a calendar		

会話を読んで、間接話法を完成させるにもっとも適した動詞を選びましょう。

1.

Mike: I didn't take your phone, I swear!

Jane: I'm not sure I believe you.

Jane _____ doubt towards Mike's words.

 A. expressed

 B. denied

 C. rebutted

 D. proposed

2.

Anna: I am sure the event will be cancelled due to the storm.

Ben: That's not true; the organizers said it would continue as planned.

Ben _____ Anna's statement.

 A. confirmed

 B. rebutted

 C. proposed

 D. admitted

3.

Trisha: The meeting will start at 10 am, not a minute later.

Oliver: Actually, the email says it will start at 10:30 am.

Oliver _____ Trisha's information.

 A. corroborated

 B. denied

 C. corrected

 D. proposed

4.

Sarah: I will never be able to complete this project on time.

Kevin: I know you can do it, just believe in yourself.

Kevin _____ Sarah's pessimism.

    A. shared

    B. dismissed

    C. emphasized

    D. confirmed

5.

David: I promise, I'll repay the loan within a month.

Rita: You better, I am counting on your word.

Rita _____ in David's promise.

    A. cast doubt

    B. believed

    C. proposed

    D. denied

Unit 14

文を完成させるにもっとも適した語句を選びましょう。

1. In the middle of the heatwave, the sale of air conditioners _____.

    A. declined

    B. soared

    C. shrunk

    D. decreased

2. After the severe storm, the number of tourists in the seaside town
   _____ dramatically.
   A. surged
   B. expanded
   C. decreased
   D. soared

3. Due to the introduction of new technology, the company's production
   capacity _____ in the last year.
   A. surged
   B. shrank
   C. dropped
   D. decreased

4. The announcement of tax increases negatively affected investor
   sentiment, and the stock market _____.
   A. soared
   B. spiked
   C. plummeted
   D. surged

5. Despite the economic recovery, the unemployment rate has _____
   over the past few months.
   A. soared
   B. spiked
   C. remained stable
   D. surged

6. Due to better healthcare facilities, the average lifespan in the country has _____ in the past decade.
   A. expanded
   B. dropped
   C. declined
   D. decreased

7. Following the negative reviews, the sales of the product _____.
   A. spiked
   B. rose
   C. surged
   D. plummeted

8. Due to an improved marketing strategy, the brand's popularity has _____ in recent years.
   A. shrunk
   B. decreased
   C. soared
   D. declined

9. After several years of drought, the lake's water level _____ significantly.
   A. expanded
   B. surged
   C. dropped
   D. spiked

10. Following a successful advertising campaign, the company's market share _____ in a short period.
   A. dropped
   B. expanded
   C. decreased
   D. declined

Answers

問題解答

Unit 1　ディスカッション表現

(Task 1)

1. disadvantage / drawback / negative aspect
2. (1) disadvantage / drawback / negative aspect
   (2) advantage / benefit
   (3) disadvantage / drawback
3. (1) pro　con　　(2) disadvantage　　(3) drawback　　(4) benefit
4. downside / disadvantage
5. drawback / downside / negative aspect

(Task 2)

1. **◀) u0101** I see a lot of advantages to hiring Ms. Svenson in the accounting department. What could be some potential drawbacks?

   スヴェンソンさんを会計部門に雇うことには多くの利点があると思います。潜在的なデメリットには何があるでしょうか?

   B. I honestly don't see any negative aspects to hiring her.

   正直なところ、彼女を雇うことに関してネガティブな側面は見あたりません。

2. **◀) u0102** Why did the WDG Group build their new plant in Poland?

   WDG グループはなぜポーランドに新しい工場を建設したのでしょうか?

   A. I think it is because Poland offers many strategic advantages to foreign investors.

   ポーランドが外国の投資家に多くの戦略的な利点を提供しているからだと思います。

3. **◀) u0103** What made you decide against buying a new car?

   何が理由で、新しい車を買わないことにしたのですか?

   C. The running cost is a major drawback, to be honest.

   正直なところ、維持費が大きな難ですね。

4. ◀)) u0104 I'm not surprised that the CEO decided not to support the new marketing plan.

CEO が新しいマーケティング計画を支持しないと決めたのは驚くに当たらないと思います。

B. I know what you mean. The disadvantages clearly outweighed the advantages.

わかります。明らかにデメリットがメリットを上回っています。

5. ◀)) u0105 Can you think of any negative aspects of participating in the project?

このプロジェクトに参加することのマイナス面を何か思いつきますか？

A. Yes, the time commitment such a project requires is a significant drawback for me.

はい、このようなプロジェクトが要求する時間的な拘束は、私にとってかなりのデメリットです。

────────── (Task 3) ──────────

◀)) u0106

At the moment we are considering two possible locations for the new plant: Bangladesh and Taiwan. We need to discuss the **pros and cons** of both options, and make a decision soon. While both Bangladesh and Taiwan offer **unique benefits** for us, I believe that Taiwan is the better option. Other members of the board believe that Bangladesh is better because it **offers the advantage of** lower labor cost. In my opinion the **main benefit** of choosing Taiwan would be the access to skilled labor that it offers. And skilled workers will give us a **competitive advantage** that cannot be matched by Bangladesh. What do you think?

現在、新工場の候補地を 2 つ検討しています。バングラデシュと台湾です。両者の長所と短所を議論し、早急に決断する必要があります。バングラデシュも台湾も、それぞれ私たちにとってメリットがありますが、私は台湾の方が良いと思っています。取締役会の他のメンバーは、労働コストがより低いという利点があるため、バングラデシュの方が良いと考えています。私の意見では、台湾を選択する最大のメリットは、熟練した労働力へのアクセスが可能になることです。熟練した労働者は、バングラデシュにはない競争上の優位性をもたらしてくれます。みなさんはどう思いますか？

1. What is the main topic of the talk?

   トークの主なトピックは何ですか?

   B. Discussing where to construct a new plant.

   新しい工場をどこに建設するかについて議論すること。

2. Why do some people believe that Bangladesh is a better option?

   なぜ一部の人々はバングラデシュがより良い選択肢だと考えているのですか?

   A. Because it offers access to cheaper labor.

   より安価な労働力へのアクセスを提供しているから。

3. What does the speaker believe about Taiwan?

   話者は台湾についてどう考えていますか?

   B. It has more skilled workers than Bangladesh

   技術力のある労働者がバングラデシュよりも多い。

4. What has to happen soon?

   近々何をしなくてはならないですか?

   C. They need to make a decision

   決定を下さなければならない。

Unit 2　因果関係表現 ①

Task 1

1. Insufficient sleep results in decreased efficiency during the day.

   不十分な睡眠は、昼間の効率の低下をもたらします。

   ↻ **Decreased efficiency during the day is caused by insufficient sleep.**

   昼間の効率の低下は、不十分な睡眠によって引き起こされます。

2. "Smartphone neck" is a pain in the neck caused by looking at a smartphone screen for a prolonged period of time.

「スマホ首」とは、長時間にわたってスマートフォンの画面を見ることによって起こる首の痛みです。

↩ **Looking at a smartphone screen for a prolonged period of time leads to pain called "smartphone neck".**

長時間スマートフォンの画面を見続けると、「スマホ首」と呼ばれる痛みを引き起こします。

3. The rapid spread of internet connectivity can be seen as the main reason for the emergence of many online businesses.

インターネット接続の急速な拡大は、多くのオンラインビジネスの出現の主な理由と見ることができます。

↩ **The emergence of many online businesses was caused by the rapid spread of internet connectivity.**

多くのオンラインビジネスの出現は、インターネット接続の急速な拡大によって引き起こされました。

4. Eating too much sugar can cause diabetes.

砂糖の過剰摂取は、糖尿病につながることがあります。

↩ **Diabetes can be caused by eating too much sugar.**

糖尿病は、砂糖の過剰摂取によって起こることがあります。

5. Reading widely leads to better vocabulary skills.

幅広く読むことは、より良い語彙力をもたらします。

↩ **Better vocabulary skills are achieved by reading widely. Better vocabulary skills are the result of reading widely.**

より良い語彙力は、幅広く読むことによって獲得できます。より良い語彙力は、幅広く読んだことの結果です。

6. Singing for hours may cause pain in the throat.

何時間も歌うことは、喉の痛みを引き起こす可能性があります。

↩ **Pain in the throat may be attributed to singing for hours.**

喉の痛みは、何時間も歌うことに起因する可能性があります。

1. 🔊 u0201 What causes a runny nose?

鼻水が出る原因は何ですか?

C. One reason could be allergies.

アレルギーは一因となり得ます。

2. 🔊 u0202 I was surprised to hear that their project failed.

彼らのプロジェクトが失敗したと聞いて驚きました。

B. So was I. But lack of funding might have caused them to fail.

私もです。ですが、資金不足が失敗の原因となったかもしれません。

3. 🔊 u0203 Why does increased sugar consumption lead to diabetes?

砂糖の大量摂取はなぜ糖尿病につながるのですか?

A. It leads to "insulin resistance", which causes diabetes.

「インスリン耐性」につながり、それが糖尿病を引き起こします。

4. 🔊 u0204 My legs are really sore; it hurts when I walk.

脚がひどく痛い。歩くと痛むんだ。

C. Typically, muscle soreness is caused by overworking the muscles. Didn't you go for a run yesterday?

ありがちなのは、筋肉痛は筋肉の使い過ぎで起こるんだ。昨日、ランニングに行っていない?

5. 🔊 u0205 Did you hear about the forest fire? It seems awful!

山火事のニュースを聞いた? 本当にひどいみたいだよ!

B. Yes, they said on the news it was caused by a lightning strike.

聞いたよ、ニュースで落雷が原因だと言っていた。

3.1. 🔊 u0206

Excessive consumption of sugar **leads to** many harmful effects on human health. The sugar intake of people in developed countries has been increasing since the second half of the 20th century. This is **seen as one of the main reasons** for the so-called obesity pandemic. The spread of obesity, in turn, **has caused** a number of diseases and conditions. In addition to being the **main cause** for type 2 diabetes, obesity is regarded **as a major driver** behind the surge in cancer, heart disease, and other serious conditions.

砂糖の過剰摂取は、人の健康に多くの悪影響を及ぼします。先進国の人々の糖分摂取量は、20世紀後半から増加しています。これは、いわゆる肥満パンデミックの主な原因の1つと考えられています。肥満の拡大は、さまざまな病気を引き起こす原因となっています。2型糖尿病の主因となっているほか、がんや心臓病その他の重い疾患の急増にも肥満が大きく影響していると考えられています。

解答・訳・解説

3.2.

1. What is the main topic of the talk?

   トークの主題は何ですか?

   C. How sugar is harmful to the human body.

   砂糖は人体にどのように有害か。

2. Which of the following is true about sugar intake?

   以下のうち、砂糖摂取に関して真実であるのはどれですか?

   A. It has been on the rise since the second half of the 20th century.

   20世紀の後半から増加してきている。

3. Obesity is mentioned as the main cause of which disease?

   肥満はどの病気の主要な原因として言及されていますか?

   B. type 2 diabetes

   2型糖尿病

4. What is the author's opinion of sugar?

著者の砂糖に関する意見はどれですか?

C. The author sees sugar as a major health hazard.

著者は砂糖を重大な健康リスクと見なしている。

Unit 3　因果関係表現 ②

Task 1

1.1. 〜 7.2.　（※解答例です）

The heavy rainfall caused severe flooding in the city.

激しい雨が都市部で深刻な洪水を引き起こしました。

The severe flooding in the city was caused by the heavy rainfall.

都市部の深刻な洪水が激しい雨によって発生しました。

Due to the lack of sleep, she felt groggy and unproductive throughout the day.

睡眠不足のため、彼女は一日中ぼんやりして生産性が低かったです。

She felt groggy and unproductive throughout the day because lacked sleep.

彼女は一日中ぼんやりして生産性が低かった、というのも、睡眠不足だったからです。

The teacher's strict grading policies can be seen as the cause for the students' high levels of stress.

教師の厳しい採点方針は、学生たちの高いストレスレベルの原因と見なすことができます。

The students' high levels of stress are due to the teacher's strict grading policies.

学生たちの高いストレスレベルは、教師の厳しい採点方針のせいです。

Thanks to her dedication and hard work, she was promoted to manager.

ひたむきな頑張りが実を結び、彼女はマネージャーに昇進しました。

Her promotion to manager was due to her dedication and hard work.

彼女がマネージャーへ昇進したのは、自身の献身と努力のおかげです。

The company's decision to cut costs resulted in the layoff of several employees.

会社がコスト削減を決定したことで、従業員が何人か解雇されました。

The layoff of several employees was a result of the company's decision to cut costs.

何人かの従業員の解雇は、コスト削減という会社の決定の結果でした。

The excessive use of technology has been shown to produce negative effects on mental health.

過剰なテクノロジーの使用は、精神的健康に否定的な影響を与えることが示されています。

Negative effects on mental health are due to the excessive use of technology.

精神的健康への否定的な影響は、過剰なテクノロジーの使用のせいです。

The widespread use of pesticides has led to a decline in bee populations.

農薬の広範な使用は、蜂の個体数の減少を引き起こしました。

The decline in bee populations is due to the widespread use of pesticides.

蜂の個体数の減少は、農薬の広範な使用のせいです。

 Task 2

1. Thanks to advancements in AI technology, self-driving cars are now able to navigate roads safely and efficiently.

    AI 技術の進歩のおかげで、自動運転車は今や道路を安全かつ効率的に走行することが可能となりました。

    ↻ Self-driving cars are now able to navigate roads safely and efficiently as a result of the advancements in AI technology.

    自動運転車は AI 技術の進歩により今や安全かつ効率的に道路を走行できるようになりました。

2. The high demand for electric vehicles has led to an increase in the production of lithium-ion batteries.

電気自動車への高い需要は、リチウムイオンバッテリーの生産増加を引き起こしています。

↻ **The increase in the production of lithium-ion batteries was caused by the high demand for electric vehicles.**

リチウムイオンバッテリーの生産が電気自動車の需要の高まりによって増加しています。

3. The development of advanced sensors has produced more accurate weather forecasting models.

高度なセンサーの開発は、より正確な天気予報モデルを生み出しています。

↻ **More accurate weather forecasting models can be attributed to the development of advanced sensors.**

より正確な天気予報モデルは高度なセンサーの開発によるものと言えます。

4. The recent surge in cryptocurrency prices can be attributed to the increasing popularity of blockchain technology.

最近の仮想通貨の価格急騰はブロックチェーン技術の人気増加に起因すると言えます。

↻ **The increasing popularity of blockchain technology can be seen as the cause for the recent surge in cryptocurrency prices.**

ブロックチェーン技術の人気の高まりは最近の仮想通貨の価格急騰をもたらしたとされています。

5. The decrease in the use of fossil fuels has been brought about by the rising concern for climate change.

化石燃料の使用量減少は、気候変動に対する懸念の高まりによって引き起こされています。

↻ **The rising concern for climate change caused the decrease in the use of fossil fuels.**

気候変動に対する懸念の高まりは化石燃料の使用量減少をもたらしました。

Unit 4 　比較表現

---------- (Task 1) ----------

1. After I reviewed the results, I wasn't (B) **as confident as** before.
   結果を見直してからは、以前ほど自信を持てませんでした。

2. Learning how to communicate effectively is much (B) **more important** than having a vast knowledge of information.
   効果的にコミュニケーションを取る方法を学ぶことは、多くの情報を知っていることよりもはるかに重要です。

3. Although the new smartphone has a (C) **slightly bigger** screen than its predecessor, their overall dimensions are still comparable.
   新しいスマートフォンは前モデルよりもわずかに画面が大きいものの、全体的な寸法はまだ比較可能です。

4. Learning a new language as an adult is much (A) **more difficult** than learning it as a child.
   大人になってから新しい言語を学ぶことは、子供時代に学ぶよりもはるかに困難です。

5. Running a marathon was not (B) **as hard as** I imagined it would be, thanks to my rigorous training regimen.
   マラソンを走ることは、厳しいトレーニングメニューのおかげで想像していたほど困難ではありませんでした。

6. The group exposed to the highest concentration of the chemical in the experiment showed (A) **twice as much** adverse effects as the group exposed to the lowest concentration.
   実験では化学物質の最も高い濃度に曝露された群は、最も低い濃度に曝露された群の 2 倍の有害な作用を示しました。

1. Poland has **the highest** percentage of university graduates among these countries.

    ポーランドは大学卒業者の割合がこれらの国の中で最も高い。

2. Greece has **the same** percentage of university graduates as Australia.

    ギリシャはオーストラリアと同じ割合の大学卒業者を有している。

3. Indonesia has **a significantly lower** percentage of university graduates, compared to Slovenia.

    インドネシアは、スロベニアと比較して大学卒業者の割合が著しく低い。

4. The percentage of university graduates in Brazil is **higher than** Indonesia.

    ブラジルの大学卒業者の割合は、インドネシアよりも高い。

5. Saudi Arabia's percentage is **significantly lower** compared to Poland.

    サウジアラビアの割合は、ポーランドに比べて著しく低い。

6. The percentage of Spain is **lower** than that of Slovenia.

    スペインの割合はスロベニアのそれよりも低い。

7. Australia and Greece both have a **higher** percentage of university graduates than Brazil.

    オーストラリアとギリシャは、ブラジルよりも大学卒業者の割合が高い。

8. Saudi Arabia's percentage is **more than** double compared to Indonesia.

    サウジアラビアの割合は、インドネシアと比較して 2 倍以上である。

1. 🔊 u0401

Man: Is this dress more expensive than the one you tried on before?

Woman: Yes, it costs twice as much.

Question: How much more expensive is the dress?

男性：これはこの前試着したドレスよりも高い?

女性：ええ、倍の値段ね。

質問：ドレスはどのくらい高価ですか?

C. The dress is twice as expensive.

そのドレスは 2 倍の価格です。

2. 🔊 u0402

Man: Do you think our team will win by a large margin?

Woman: No, it will be a slightly closer game than last time.

Question: How does the woman think the game will be?

男性：うちのチームは大差で勝つと思う?

女性：いいえ、前回より少しは接戦になるでしょう。

質問：女性はどのような試合になると思っていますか?

B. The game will be slightly closer than the previous one.

前回の試合よりも点差はわずかに近づくだろう。

3. 🔊 u0403

Woman: Is the new laptop faster than the old one?

Man: Yes, it's significantly more powerful.

Question: What does the man think of the new laptop?

女性：新しいノートパソコンは古いものより速いですか?

男性：はい、かなりパワフルです。

質問：男性は新しいノートパソコンについてどう思っていますか?

A. The new laptop is significantly more powerful than the old one.

新しいノートパソコンは古いものよりもかなりパワフルである。

4. u0404

Man: Is the traffic in LA worse than in Chattanooga?

Woman: Yes, it's much more congested.

Question: How does the woman feel about the traffic in LA?

男性：LA の交通はチャタヌーガよりもひどいですか?

女性：はい、はるかに混雑しています。

質問：女性は LA の交通についてどう感じていますか?

C. The traffic is significantly worse in LA.

交通状況は LA の方が著しく悪い。

5. u0405

Man: Austin and Phoenix are comparable, aren't they?

Woman: Yes, the population is almost the same.

Question: What does the woman mean?

男性：オースティンとフェニックスは比較の対象になりますよね?

女性：はい、人口はほぼ同じです。

質問：女性は何が言いたいのでしょうか?

B. Austin is as big as Phoenix in terms of population.

オースティンはフェニックスと同じくらい人口があります。

Unit 5　if/when/wish　現実と架空

・(Task 1)・
---

1. During the meeting yesterday I was supposed to present my marketing ideas about the new product. I had nothing to say, and I was so embarrassed. I wish I **had prepared** for the meeting.

   昨日の会議で新製品に関するマーケティングのアイデアを発表する予定でした。言うことが何もなくて、とても恥ずかしい思いをしました。会議の準備をしておけばよかったです。

2. What **would you say** if you could talk to the President of the United States?

   アメリカの大統領と話せるとしたら、どんなことを言いますか?

3. I would buy this house if it **were** less expensive.

   この家がもっと安ければ、買うのですが。

4. If I had had more time, I **would have studied** more for my exams.

   もっと時間があれば、試験のためにもっと勉強したのですが。

5. If she **were** taller, she could reach the top shelf.

   彼女がもっと背が高ければ、最上段に手が届くのですが。

6. If it **rains** tomorrow, I won't go to the park.

   明日雨が降ったら、公園には行きません。

7. If he **had** a car, he could drive us to the beach.

   もし彼が車を持っていれば、私たちをビーチまで乗せてくれるのですが。

8. If we **had left** early, we could have beaten the traffic.

   早く出発していれば、渋滞にあわずに済んだのですが。

9. If they **had met** earlier, they could have gone to the concert together.

   もし彼らが早く合流できていれば、一緒にコンサートに行けたのですが。

10. If I **won** the lottery, I would travel the world.

    もし宝くじが当たれば、世界中を旅行するのですが。

11. If you **had listened** to me, you wouldn't have made that mistake.

    私の言うことを聞いていれば、そのミスをしなかったでしょうに。

12. If the weather **were** better, we could have a picnic.

天気が良ければ、ピクニックができるのですが。

13. If she **spoke** Spanish, she could communicate better with her grandmother.

彼女がスペイン語を話せれば、祖母ともっとうまくコミュニケーションが取れるのですが。

14. If she **liked** spicy food, I would recommend this dish to her.

彼女が辛い食べ物が好きなら、この料理を彼女に勧めるのですが。

15. If he **had known** the answer, he would have raised his hand.

彼が答えを知っていれば、手を挙げたのですが。

16. If we **had arrived** earlier, we could have watched the whole movie.

早く到着していれば、映画を最初から見ることができたのですが。

17. If they **finish** their work, they can go home early.

仕事を終えれば、彼らは早く帰宅できます。

18. If I **had** a magic wand, I would make everyone happy.

魔法の杖を持っていれば、皆を幸せにするのですが。

19. If the sky **is** clear tonight, we will see the solar eclipse.

今夜空が晴れていれば、日食が見られるでしょう。

Task 2

1. I'll go to the store **when** I have time.

時間があるときにお店に行きます。

2. **If** it rains, we'll stay inside.

雨が降ったら、中にいましょう。

3. I'll call you **when** I arrive at the airport.

   空港に着いたらお電話します。

4. **If** you need help, just ask.

   助けが必要なら、聞いてください。

5. **When** I see her, I'll give her the message.

   彼女に会ったら、そのメッセージを伝えます。

6. We'll have a party **when** we finish the project.

   プロジェクトが終わったらパーティーを開きます。

7. I would help you **if** I could.

   できるなら手伝いたいです。

8. I'll buy a new car **when** I have enough money.

   お金が十分にあるときに新しい車を買います。

9. **If** I finish my homework by 8, I'll watch a movie.

   宿題が 8 時までに終わったら、映画を見ます。

10. **When** you finish your dinner, we can go for a walk.

    夕食が終わったら、散歩に行きましょう。

11. **When** you're ready, let's start the presentation.

    用意ができたら、プレゼンテーションを始めましょう。

12. **If** she arrives earlier than 5 pm, please give me a call.

    彼女が午後 5 時より早く到着したら、私に電話してください。

Unit 6 ifを使わない条件表現

Task 1

Sentence	Correct	Incorrect
1. I always carry a spare tire in my trunk, provided I get a flat on the road.		○ provided → in case
2. In case of a power outage, the backup generator will automatically kick in to keep the lights on.	○	
3. I will email you a copy of the report as long as you need it for your records.		○ as long as → in case
4. You can use the company car provided that you follow the rules and regulations.	○	
5. Providing you need to contact me during the trip, my cell phone will have international roaming enabled.		○ Providing → If
6. I will lend you the money in case you pay me back within a month.		○ in case → as long as
7. The discount is valid provided that you present this coupon at the time of purchase.	○	
8. As long as there are no technical difficulties, the online class should run smoothly.	○	
9. In case you study hard, you will do well on the exam.		○ as long as → provided
10.I will continue to support you as long as you make a genuine effort to change.	○	

Task 2

1. 🔊 u0601 He told me the truth, so I wasn't in the dark.

    彼は私に真実を言ってくれたので、私は手探り状態ではありませんでした。

    A. If he hadn't told me the truth, I would still have been in the dark.

    もし彼が私に真実を言ってくれなかったら、まだ手探り状態だったでしょう。

2. **◀)) u0602** I made a costly mistake because I wasn't informed.

情報が不足していたので、高くつくミスをしました。

C. Had I been more informed, I wouldn't have made such a costly mistake.

もっと情報を持っていたら、そんな高くつくミスをしなかったでしょう。

3. **◀)) u0603** He met his future wife because he took that job.

彼はその仕事を受けたので、未来の奥さんに会いました。

B. If he hadn't taken that job, he wouldn't have met his future wife.

もし彼がその仕事を受けなかったら、未来の奥さんには会えなかったでしょう。

4. **◀)) u0604** We want you to let us know immediately if you change your plans.

予定を変更することになったら、すぐにお知らせください。

A. Should you decide to change your plans, let us know as soon as possible.

予定を変更することに決めたら、できるだけ早くお知らせください。

5. **◀)) u0605** We would appreciate your feedback on our proposal, if you have time.

お時間があれば、私たちの提案に関するフィードバックをいただけると幸いです。

B. Should you have time, we would appreciate your feedback on our proposal.

お時間があれば、私たちの提案に関するフィードバックをいただけると感謝します。

6. **◀)) u0606** If we hadn't gone to that museum, we wouldn't have discovered that new artist.

もし私たちがその美術館に行かなかったら、その新しいアーティストを発見することはありませんでした。

C. It's great that we went to that museum. Otherwise, we wouldn't have discovered that new artist.

その美術館に行ってよかったです。さもなければ、その新しいアーティストを発見できなかったでしょう。

Unit 7 質問を使った表現

---• (Task 1) •---

1. 🔊 u0701

Man: You should tell John. I'm sure he'll understand.

Woman: Will he, though? I broke his favorite vase!

男性：ジョンに言うべきですよ。きっと彼は理解してくれますよ。

女性：そうかな? 彼のお気に入りの花瓶を壊しちゃったんだけど!

A. John will definitely be angry.

ジョンは確実に怒るでしょう。

2. 🔊 u0702

Man: You should quit your job, and find a less stressful one.

Woman: How can you say such a thing? I love my job!

男性：仕事を辞めて、もっとストレスの少ない仕事を見つけるべきですよ。

女性：そんなことをどうして言えるの? 私、仕事が大好きなんだから!

C. She doesn't want to quit her job.

彼女は仕事を辞めたくありません。

3. 🔊 u0703

Man: It's going to rain tomorrow. We can't go hiking.

Woman: Why don't we go see a movie then?

男性：明日は雨が降るよ。ハイキングには行けないね。

女性：じゃあ、映画でも見に行かない?

B. She is proposing an alternative way to spend the day.

彼女はその日の別の過ごし方を提案しています。

4. 🔊 u0704

Man: You've bought a new car! Wow, it looks fantastic!

Woman: Oh, thank you. Why did I buy a new car when I'm between jobs? Because, guess what! I found a new job! And it's much better paying than the old one.

男性：新しい車を買ったんだね! わあ、見た目が素晴らしいね!

女性：あ、ありがとう。仕事を探している間に新しい車を買うなんて、どうしてだと思う? 実はね、新しい仕事が見つかったの! そして、前の仕事よりもずっと給料がいいんだ。

C. She has become able to afford a new car.

彼女は新しい車を買う余裕ができました。

5. 🔊 u0705

Man: I'm in real trouble. My boss is going to kill me!

Woman: Is he? I'm plently sure he won't care.

男性：本当に困ってるんだ。上司に怒られるよ!

女性：本当に? 全然気にしていないと思うよ。

B. The boss is not going to be concerned.

上司は気にしないでしょう。

 Task 2

(※解答例です)

1. Let's go to the movies tonight.

今夜、映画に行こう。

↩ Why don't we go to the movies tonight?

今夜、映画に行かない?

2. We should try that new restaurant.

その新しいレストランを試してみよう。

↩ How about trying that new restaurant?

その新しいレストランを試してみるのはどう?

3. We could have a picnic in the park this weekend.

この週末、公園でピクニックがいいかもね。

↻ **What about having a picnic in the park this weekend?**

この週末、公園でピクニックするのはどう?

4. Let's take a day off and go to the beach.

休みを取ってビーチに行こう。

↻ **How about taking a day off and going to the beach?**

休みを取ってビーチに行くのはどう?

5. We should visit our grandparents this Sunday.

今週の日曜日、おじいちゃんおばあちゃんを訪ねるべきだ。

↻ **What about visiting our grandparents this Sunday?**

今週の日曜日、おじいちゃんおばあちゃんを訪ねるのはどう?

6. Let's make a homemade pizza for dinner.

夕食に自家製のピザを作ろう。

↻ **Why don't we make a homemade pizza for dinner?**

夕食に自家製のピザを作らない?

7. We could organize a game night at our place.

家でゲーム・ナイトをやるといいかもね。

↻ **How about organizing a game night at our place?**

家でゲーム・ナイトをやるのはどう?

8. Let's go for a hike in the mountains.

山にハイキングに行こう。

↻ **What about going for a hike in the mountains?**

山にハイキングに行くのはどう?

9. We should plan a weekend getaway.

   週末の小旅行を計画するべきだ。

   ↻ **Why don't we plan a weekend getaway?**

   週末の小旅行を計画しない?

10. Let's have a barbecue party in our backyard.

    裏庭でバーベキューパーティーをしよう。

    ↻ **How about having a barbecue party in our backyard?**

    裏庭でバーベキューパーティーをするのはどう?

Unit 8　情報の提供・追加表現

・(Task 1)・

1. The data collected in this study indicate that exercise can improve cognitive function. Moreover, (A) **it was also found to have a positive impact on mood.**

   この研究で収集されたデータは、運動が認知機能を向上させることを示しています。さらに、気分にも良い影響を与えることが分かりました。

B. other experts in the field have expressed concerns regarding the quality of the data. や C. 25% of the participants reported disruption in sleep. は、moreover の後ろには自然に続かないことがわかります。On the other hand や however であれば B や C は正解になり得ます。

2. This report presents an analysis of the company's financial performance for the last quarter. In addition, (A) **the report also includes a breakdown of the sales figures by product category.**

   この報告書は、過去四半期の企業の財務実績の分析を提示しています。加えて、報告書には製品カテゴリー別の売上高の内訳も含まれています。

213

B および C は、話題を変えているので、In addition に続く文としては適切ではありません。

3. This article discusses the benefits of meditation for mental health. By the way, (B) **I read in another article that meditation is also very helpful for improving concentration and productivity.**

   この記事は瞑想が精神衛生にもたらす利点について議論しています。ところで、別の記事で読んだのですが、瞑想は集中力と生産性を向上させるのにも非常に役立つと言われています。

A は、Furthermore など同じ流れの追加情報なら良い選択ですが、「それはそうと」で続ける内容ではありません。C は、テーマを維持しながら、違った方向性（ネガティブな情報）の情報を与えているため、However などに続けるには良いですが、By the way の続きとしては適しません。

4. David's presentation outlined the main features of the new software program our company released last month. What's more, (A) **he also included a demo of the software in action.**

   デイビッドのプレゼンテーションは、当社が先月リリースした新しいソフトウェアプログラムの主要な機能を概説しました。さらに、彼はソフトウェアのデモンストレーションも含めました。

B はあまりにも本題からかけ離れているので、What's more で接続すると支離滅裂になってしまいます。C は、By the way の続きとしてならば適していますが、What's more で続けるには合いません。

5. Muramoto's new novel explores the themes of love and loss in a unique and engaging way. Another aspect of the novel (A) **that deserves attention is its use of humor to lighten the mood.**

   村本さんの新しい小説は、独特かつ魅力的な方法で愛と喪失というテーマを探求しています。この小説のもう一つの注目すべき側面は、雰囲気を和らげるためのユーモアの使用です。

B と C は、Another aspect of the novel の続きとして不適です。B は商業的な成功に話題が移っていること、C は小説を肯定している前文と矛盾する上、小説を描写する内容ではないことがその理由です。

Unit 9　対照・否定表現

——・(Task 1)・——

1. 🔊 u0901

The weather is awful but I really want to go skiing!

天気はひどいけど、本当にスキーに行きたいんだ!

B. We should go regardless.

そんなの気にしないで、行こうよ(悪天候にも関わらず、行くべきです)。

2. 🔊 u0902

How are the Mayan pyramids in Mexico different from the Egyptian pyramids?

メキシコのマヤピラミッドはエジプトのピラミッドとどう違いますか?

A. We know a lot about the Egyptian ones, whereas we are just starting to explore the ones in Mexico.

エジプトのものについてはわかっていることがたくさんありますが、メキシコのものについてはまだ調査を始めたばかりです。

3. 🔊 u0903

I don't want to go to Tim's party – it's raining, and it's cold.

ティムのパーティー行きたくないなあ。雨降ってるし、それに寒いし。

C. He's our friend, we should go regardless.

友達だろ? 雨なんかいいから行こうよ(彼は私たちの友人です、雨にも関わらず行くべきです)。

4. 🔊 u0904

You should definitely buy this house! It's magnificent!

この家を絶対に買うべきです! 素晴らしいですよ!

B. Still, I'm not convinced it's worth investing so much money.

それでも、そんなに多くのお金を投資する価値があるようには思えません。

5. 🔊 u0905

Is Jane as difficult as they say she is?

ジェーンは言われているほど扱いにくいですか?

B. On the contrary, I think she's lovely.

   そんなことはないです、逆に、彼女はとても素敵だと思います。

6. 🔊 u0906

You should definitely go out with John. He's good-looking, and also, he's the captain of the baseball team. Not only that, he's a super smart guy!

ジョンとデートするべきだよ。見た目はいいし、それに、野球チームのキャプテンだよ。その上、頭だってものすごくいいんだ!

A. Regardless of all of that, I don't date sporty guys.

   そういうの全部関係なくて、私は運動系の男性とはデートしません。

7. 🔊 u0907

I called you 7 times yesterday! Where were you?

昨日は 7 回もあなたに電話しましたよ! どこにいたんですか?

C. I'm sorry. But I was with a client.

   申し訳ありません。でも、クライアントと一緒だったんです。

 Task 2

1. 🔊 u0908

The company's revenues have been steadily increasing, but expenses have also been on the rise. Thus, (1) A. **despite** the increase in revenues, the company's profit margins have been declining.

(2) B. **However**, the company has implemented cost-saving measures to offset the impact of rising expenses.

(3) C. **In contrast**, competitors in the market have managed to maintain higher profit margins by optimizing their operational costs.

(4) A. **Nevertheless** the company's strong brand presence and loyal customer base have helped mitigate the effects of the declining profit margins.

会社の収益は着実に増加していますが、支出も増加しています。したがって、収益の増加にもかかわらず、会社の利益率は低下しています。

しかし、会社は支出の増加の影響を相殺するためのコスト削減策を実施しています。

対照的に、市場の競合他社は運営コストの最適化によって高い利益率を維持することに成功しています。

それでも、会社の強力なブランドプレゼンスと忠実な顧客基盤が利益率の低下の影響を緩和するのに役立っています。

解答・訳・解説

2. 🔊 u0909

Our university's research team has made significant progress in cancer treatment.

(1) C. **On top of that**, the experimental drug has shown promising results in shrinking tumor sizes in early-stage clinical trials.

(2) B. **Yet another** breakthrough in the field of oncology is the development of personalized treatment plans based on genetic profiling.

(3) A. **One more** exciting development is the use of immunotherapy, which harnesses the body's immune system to fight cancer cells.

(4) A. **Moreover**, the research team is exploring the potential of targeted therapy to minimize side effects and improve patient outcomes.

私たちの大学の研究チームはがん治療において顕著な進歩を遂げました。

その上、実験薬は初期段階の臨床試験で腫瘍のサイズを縮小させる有望な結果を示しています。

また、腫瘍学分野での新たなブレイクスルーは、遺伝子プロファイリングに基づき患者個人に合わせた治療計画の開発です。

もう一つの興味深い開発は、体の免疫システムを利用してがん細胞と戦う免疫療法の使用です。

さらに、研究チームは、副作用を最小限に抑え、患者の結果を改善するためのターゲット治療の可能性を探求しています。

3. 🔊 u0910

Clark's findings support the effectiveness of traditional teaching methods, (1) A. **even though** technology is rapidly advancing.

(2) B. **Even so**, incorporating technology into education has its advantages, such as enhancing student engagement and providing interactive learning experiences.

(3) C. **Still**, many educators prefer traditional teaching methods due to their proven track record of success.

(4) B. **Conversely**, some argue that technology should be embraced in the classroom to prepare students for the digital age.

クラークの調査結果は、テクノロジーが急速に進歩しているにもかかわらず、伝統的な教授法の有効性を支持しています。

それでも、教育にテクノロジーを取り入れることには、学生の関与を高めることやインタラクティブな学習経験を提供することなど、利点があります。

とは言え、多くの教育者は、その成功の実績が証明されているため、伝統的な教授法を好んでいます。

逆に、一部の人々は、生徒がデジタル時代に備えられるように、教室でテクノロジーを積極的に活用すべきだと主張しています。

4. 🔊 u0911

Recent studies have shown the benefits of regular exercise on mental health.

(1) A. **In addition to** improving mental well-being, exercise has been linked to increased productivity at work.

(2) B. **Furthermore**, it has been found to enhance cognitive function, leading to better decision-making skills.

(3) A. Moreover, engaging in physical activity can also help reduce stress levels and promote overall work-life balance.

(4) B. Furthermore, incorporating exercise into one's routine has been shown to boost creativity and enhance problem-solving abilities.

最近の研究では、定期的な運動が精神衛生にもたらす利点が示されています。

運動は精神的な幸福感を向上させるだけでなく、職場での生産性の向上と関連があることがわかっています。

さらに、認知機能の向上が見られ、より良い意思決定能力につながることが判明しています。

加えて、身体活動に従事することは、ストレスレベルを減らし、全体的な仕事と生活のバランスを促進するのにも役立ちます。

さらに、運動を日常のルーティーンに取り入れることで、創造性を高め、問題解決能力を向上させることが示されています。

Unit 10　参照と言い換え ①

Task 1

1. Do you know that honeybees play a crucial role in pollination? Over the last few decades, **their** numbers have sharply declined, raising concerns about **their** future survival.

   蜜蜂は受粉において重要な役割を果たすことを知っていますか? その数は過去数十年にわたり急激に減少しており、将来の生存に関する懸念が高まっています。

2. The board had two important decisions to make: invest in research and development, or initiate a stock buyback program. **The former** was seen as an investment in the future, while **the latter** was a way to immediately reward shareholders.

取締役会は 2 つの重要な決定を下す必要がありました：研究と開発への投資、または株式買い戻しプログラムの開始。前者は将来への投資と見なされましたが、後者は株主に即時報酬を提供する方法でした。

3. The CEO and the CFO had a detailed discussion about the company's financial health. **They** shared **their** concerns about the rising operational costs.

CEO と CFO は、会社の財務状態について詳細な議論を行いました。彼らは運営費用の増加に関する懸念を共有しました。

4. When Lucy discovered the lost manuscript in the library, **she** felt like she had found a hidden treasure. **She** knew **its** value was immense.

図書館で失われた原稿を発見したとき、ルーシーは隠された宝を見つけたような気がしました。その価値が莫大であることを彼女は知っていました。

5. The architect and the builder had a debate about the design of the house. **The former** argued for a modern design, while **the latter** preferred a more traditional approach. In the end, **they** decided to ask Jack, the owner of the house, about **his** preference.

建築家と建築業者は家のデザインについて議論しました。前者はモダンなデザインを主張しましたが、後者はもっと伝統的なアプローチを好みました。最終的に、彼らは家のオーナーであるジャックに好みを尋ねることに決めました。

6. William Shakespeare didn't go to university. However, after **his** schooling, **he** wrote some of the most celebrated works in the English language.

ウィリアム・シェイクスピアは大学には行きませんでした。しかし、学校教育が終わった後、彼は英語で最も称賛される作品のいくつかを書きました。

7. The human body has millions of neurons. **They** transmit information between different parts of the body, playing a crucial role in **its** ability to sense and respond to the environment.

    人体には数百万のニューロンがあります。これらは体の異なる部分間で情報を伝達し、環境を感知し反応する能力において重要な役割を果たします。

8. After a long meeting, the marketing team and the sales team finally reached a consensus. **They** decided to jointly launch a new campaign, with **the former** focusing on online promotions and **the latter** focusing on direct customer engagement.

    長い会議の後、マーケティングチームとセールスチームはついに合意に達しました。彼らは新しいキャンペーンを共同で立ち上げることを決定しました。前者はオンラインプロモーションに焦点を当て、後者は直接の顧客エンゲージメントに焦点を当てます。

Task 2

In the mid-1940s, Chester Carlson, a patent attorney with a knack for engineering, found himself exhausted with the manual process of producing multiple copies of documents. This struggle inspired **him** to experiment in **his** kitchen, leading to a revolutionary invention that we now know as the photocopier.

His first attempts were unsuccessful. Using static electricity, **he** tried to attract dry particles of ink onto a piece of paper, but it resulted in a mess. Yet, **he** was not deterred. He persisted, recognizing the potential of **his** concept. His latter attempts included a more refined version of **his** initial strategy. This time, **he** succeeded in creating a legible copy of a text on a slide. **He** called the process "xerography", derived from the Greek words for "dry" and "writing".

However, the journey of transforming **his** invention into a commercial product was challenging. **He** struggled to find a company willing to invest in **it**. The first 20 firms he approached rejected **his** proposal, unable to see the potential. Eventually, the Haloid Company, later known as Xerox, decided to take a risk and backed his idea. **Their** gamble paid off, and the photocopier became a cornerstone of the modern office.

The impact of Carlson's invention was profound. **It** transformed the dynamics of paperwork, enabling businesses to reproduce documents quickly and efficiently. In spite of the initial hurdles, **his** determination led to a breakthrough that has left its mark on our daily lives.

1940 年代半ば、エンジニアリングに長けた弁理士であるチェスター・カールソンは、書類を何枚も手で書き写すことに疲弊していた。奮闘の末、台所で実験してみようと思い立った。これが、現在のコピー機の原型となる画期的な発明につながった。

カールソンの最初の試みはうまくいかなかった。静電気を利用して、乾いたインクの粒を紙の上に吸着させようとしたが、散々な結果になってしまった。だが彼は諦めなかった。アイデアには実現の見込みがあると信じて、根気強く続けた。改良を加えながら、より洗練されたバージョンを作ることができた。今度は、スライドに文章を写すことに成功した。ギリシャ語の「乾く」と「書く」に由来するこのプロセスを「ゼログラフィー」と名付けた。

しかし、この発明を商品化するまでの道のりは険しいものだった。投資してくれる企業を探すのに苦労した。最初にアプローチした 20 社は、可能性を見いだせず、彼の提案を却下した。そんな中、ハロイド社（後のゼロックス社）がリスクを取って、彼のアイデアを支援してくれた。その賭けが功を奏し、この発明は現代のオフィスの基礎となった。

カールソンの発明による影響は目を見張るものだった。ペーパーワークの在り方を変え、企業が文書を迅速かつ効率的に再現することを可能にした。当初の困難にもかかわらず、彼の決意は、私たちの日常生活を大きく変える画期的な発明へとつながった。

Unit 11　参照と言い換え ②

---・(Task 1)・---

（※解答例です）

word	category	application/location/details
pipette	is a piece of lab equipment	used to transfer small volumes of liquid
engine	is a machine	that converts energy into mechanical power to perform tasks
hammer	is a tool	used for striking or driving nails
CAD software	is a type of software	used to create or modify designs in a digital format
petri dish	is a piece of lab equipment	used for culturing and observing microorganisms
helium	is an odorless gas	used in scientific research, medical imaging, and industrial processes
bulldozer	is a piece of heavy machinery	used for pushing and leveling earth, debris, or other materials
gravity	is a concept in physics representing	a natural force of attraction that exists between objects with mass, causing them to move toward each other
optical mouse	is a computer peripheral	that uses optical sensors to detect surface movements, providing input to the computer
steam roller	is a piece of construction equipment	used for compacting and leveling surfaces
seminar	is an educational event	where a group of individuals gathers to discuss and exchange knowledge on a specific topic or subject
chess	is a board game	played on a checkered gameboard with 64 squares arranged in an 8x8 grid

単語	カテゴリー	応用 / 場所 / 詳細
ピペット	は実験室の器具で	小量の液体を移すために使用されます
エンジン	は機械で	エネルギーを機械的動力に変換し、タスクを実行するために使用されます
ハンマー	は工具で	釘を打つまたは打ち込むために使用されます
CAD ソフトウェア	はソフトウェアの一種で	デジタルフォーマットでデザインを作成、または変更するために使用されます
ペトリ皿	は実験室の器具で	微生物を培養し観察するために使用されます
ヘリウム	は無臭のガスで	科学研究、医療画像診断、および工業で使用されます
ブルドーザー	は重機の一種で	土、瓦礫、または他の材料を押したり、平らにしたりするために使用されます
重力	は物理学の概念で	質量を持つ物体間に存在する、互いに引き寄せる自然の力を表します
光学マウス	はコンピュータ周辺機器で	光学センサーを使用して表面の動きを検出し、コンピュータに入力します
スチームローラー	は建設機械の一種で	表面を固めたり、平らにしたりするために使用されます
セミナー	は教育イベントで	特定のトピックや主題に関して知識や情報の交換や議論をグループで行なう場です
チェス	はボードゲームで	8x8 の格子型に配置された 64 マスの市松模様のゲームボードで行なわれます

Task 2

1. I absolutely <u>despise</u> the taste of mushrooms.

   キノコの味が本当に嫌いです。

   loathe　　嫌悪する

2. Sally is a(n) <u>diligent</u> student who always completes her assignments on time.

   サリーはいつも宿題を時間通りに終える、勤勉な学生です。

   conscientious　　誠実な

3. The company plans to expand its <u>operations</u> to other countries.

   その企業は他の国にも事業を拡大する計画です。

   business　　ビジネス、事業

4. Under favorable conditions, the business is likely to <u>flourish</u> and generate significant profits.

   条件が良ければ、そのビジネスは繁栄し、かなりの利益を生み出す可能性があります。

   thrive　　繁栄する

5. As I walked by the window, I <u>saw</u> the magnificent sunset.

   窓のそばを歩いているとき、壮大な夕日が見えました。

   caught a glimpse of　　ちらりと見る

6. If you have any questions, feel free to <u>ask</u> the instructor after the class.

   質問があれば、授業後に講師にお気軽にどうぞ。

   inquire with　　〜に尋ねる

(Task 3)

The invention of the Internet revolutionized global communication and information access.

From its military origins, the Internet expanded into a worldwide network, leading to the invention of the World Wide Web and its commercialization. The Internet connected people globally, facilitating collaboration and knowledge sharing.

Technological advancements, such as search engines, email, e-commerce, social media, and streaming services, further transformed the Internet's capabilities.

【要約の日本語訳】

軍事的な起源から、インターネットは世界規模のネットワークへと拡大し、それによってワールドワイドウェブが発明され、商業化されました。

検索エンジン、電子メール、電子商取引、ソーシャルメディア、およびストリーミングサービスなどの技術的進歩が、さらにインターネットの機能を変革しました。

1.　A

B と C は「マイナーなポイント」であり、全体図を伝える上で割愛しても良い内容です。

2.　B

A と C はパッセージの全体像を伝える上で有用でないというだけではなく、C はやや本題から外れています。

【パッセージの日本語訳】

20 世紀後半、私たちのつながりやコミュニケーション、情報へのアクセス方法を一変させる発明が誕生した。それがインターネットだ。1960 年代の ARPANET（Advanced Research Projects Agency Network）を起源とするインターネットは、当初、核攻撃に耐えられる分散型通信ネットワークとして開発された。

その後、インターネットは、軍事や学術的なルーツを超えて、相互に接続されたコンピュータのグローバルネットワークへと発展していった。1989 年には、ティム・バーナーズ＝リーが World Wide Web を発明し、情報へのアクセスやナビゲーションを容易にするハイパーリンクを導入した。

1990 年代にはインターネットの商業化が進み、多くのインターネットサービスプロバイダ（ISP）が設立され、Netscape Navigator や Internet Explorer などのユーザーフレンドリーなウェブブラウザが登場した。この商業化によって、インターネットはより多くの人々に開かれ、普及の道筋がつけられた。

インターネットは世界中の人々をつなぎ、地理的な境界を越えて、コミュニケーション、コラボレーション、知識の共有に革命をもたらした。それに続く技術的な進歩は、検索エンジン、電子メール、電子商取引プラットフォーム、ソーシャルメディア、ストリーミングサービスの開発という形をとった。

今日、インターネットは私たちの日常生活に欠かせないものとなっており、情報への即時アクセス、大陸を越えた垣根のないコミュニケーション、グローバルなコミュニティの醸成を可能にしている。

Unit 12　間接話法 ①

• (Task 1) •
---

1. "I will be late tonight," said John.

   「今晩遅くなる」とジョンは言いました。

   ↻ **John said that he would be late that night.**

   ジョンは、その夜遅くなるだろうと言いました。

2. "Are you okay?" Mary asked.

   「大丈夫ですか?」とメアリーが聞きました。

   ↻ **Mary asked if I was okay.**

   メアリーは私が大丈夫かどうか聞きました。

3. "I love this restaurant!" exclaimed Sarah.

   「このレストラン、大好き!」とサラが叫びました。

   ↻ **Sarah exclaimed that she loved that restaurant.**

   サラは、そのレストランが大好きだと叫びました。

4. "We need to finish the project by Friday," the manager told the team.

   「金曜日までにプロジェクトを終える必要があります」とマネージャーはチームに告げました。

   ↻ **The manager told the team that they needed to finish the project by Friday.**

   マネージャーはチームに、金曜日までにプロジェクトを終える必要があると言いました。

5. "Don't forget to pick up the laundry," Alex reminded Lisa.

   「クリーニングを取りに行くのを忘れないで」とアレックスはリサに思い出させました。

   ↻ **Alex reminded Lisa not to forget to pick up the laundry.**

   アレックスはリサに、クリーニングを取りに行くのを忘れないようにと思い出させました。

6. "I didn't steal the cookies," insisted Tom.

    「僕はクッキーを盗んでいない」とトムが主張しました。

    🔁 **Tom insisted that he hadn't stolen the cookies.**

    トムは、クッキーを盗んでいないと主張しました。

7. "I've finished my homework," Jenny told her mother.

    「宿題が終わった」とジェニーが母に告げました。

    🔁 **Jenny told her mother that she had finished her homework.**

    ジェニーは母に、宿題が終わったと言いました。

8. "Let's meet at the cinema at 7," proposed Steve.

    「7 時に映画館で会おう」とスティーブが提案しました。

    🔁 **Steve proposed meeting at the cinema at 7.**

    スティーブは 7 時に映画館で会うことを提案しました。

9. "I can't believe we won the match!" shouted Carlos.

    「試合に勝ったなんて信じられない!」とカルロスが叫びました。

    🔁 **Carlos shouted that he couldn't believe they had won the match.**

    カルロスは、試合に勝ったことが信じられないと叫びました。

10. "You should get some rest," advised Dr. Brown.

    「少し休むべきです」とブラウン先生がアドバイスしてくれました。

    🔁 **Dr. Brown advised that I should get some rest.**

    ブラウン先生は、私に少し休むべきだとアドバイスしました。

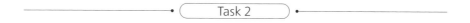

───────────●─(Task 2)─●───────────

1.

Direct: "The meeting has been postponed," she said.

直接：「会議は延期されました」と彼女は言いました。

Indirect: She **reported** that the meeting had been postponed.

間接：彼女は会議が延期されたと報告しました。

2.

Direct: "Why don't we go to the park tomorrow?" he said.

直接：「明日公園に行かない?」と彼は言いました。

Indirect: He **suggested** that we should go to the park tomorrow.

間接：彼は明日公園に行こうと提案しました。

3.

Direct: "I don't think this is fair," she said.

直接：「これは公平ではないと思う」と彼女は言いました。

Indirect: She **argued** that she didn't think it was fair.

間接：彼女はそれが公平ではないと思うと主張しました。

4.

Direct: "I've finished the report," he announced.

直接：「レポートを終えました」と彼は言いました。

Indirect: He **declared** that he had finished the report.

間接：彼はレポートを終えたと宣言しました。

5.

Direct: "The cake was delicious," they said.

直接：「ケーキはおいしかった」と彼らは言いました。

Indirect: They **commented** that the cake was delicious.

間接：彼らはケーキがおいしかったとコメントしました。

6.

Direct: "I swear I will finish the project by tomorrow!" she said.

直接：「明日までにプロジェクトを終えると誓います!」と彼女は言いました。

Indirect: She **promised** to finish the project by tomorrow.

間接：彼女は明日までにプロジェクトを終えると約束しました。

7.

Direct: "I am not responsible for the mistake," he said.

直接：「そのミスの責任は私にはありません」と彼は言いました。

Indirect: He **denied** being responsible for the mistake.

間接：彼はそのミスの責任を否定しました。

8.

Direct: "It might rain tomorrow," he said.

直接：「明日雨が降るかもしれません」と彼は言いました。

Indirect: He **mentioned** that it might rain tomorrow.

間接：彼は明日雨が降るかもしれないと言及しました。

9.

Direct: "Let's meet at 5pm," she suggested.

直接：「5 時に会いましょう」と彼女が提案しました。

Indirect: She **proposed** meeting at 5pm.

間接：彼女は 5 時に会うことを提案しました。

10.

Direct: "I can't complete this project alone," he admitted.

直接：「このプロジェクトを一人で完成させることはできない」と彼は認めました。

Indirect: He **conceded** that he couldn't complete the project alone.

間接：彼は一人でプロジェクトを完成させることができないと認めました。

1. ◀) u1201

Woman: Did you watch the new action movie with Nick Rivers?

Man: I did, and, to be honest, I wasn't impressed. All of his movies are the same.

女性：ニック・リバース主演の新しいアクション映画見ましたか？

男性：見ましたが、正直言ってそれほど良いと思いませんでした。彼の映画は全部同じですね。

A. The man told the woman that he didn't like the movie.

男性は女性に、映画が気に入らなかったと言いました。

2. ◀) u1202

Teacher: Did you do your homework, Emily?

Emily: Yes, I did. It was quite challenging but I managed to finish it.

先生：宿題やったか、エミリー？

エミリー：はい、やりました。かなり難しかったけど、何とか完成させました。

C. Emily informed the teacher that she completed the homework despite it being difficult.

エミリーは先生に、困難だったにもかかわらず宿題を終えたと報告しました。

3. ◀) u1203

Boss: How did the presentation go, Michael?

Michael: It was a disaster. The clients didn't like our proposal at all.

上司：プレゼンテーションはどうだった、マイケル？

マイケル：ひどかったです。クライアントは私たちの提案をまったく気に入らなかったようです。

B. Michael confessed to his boss that the presentation did not go well and the clients disliked their proposals.

マイケルは上司に、プレゼンテーションがうまくいかなかったし、クライアントは彼らの提案が気に入らなかったと打ち明けました。

4. 🔊 u1204

Patient: Doctor, how serious is my condition?

Doctor: I won't lie, it's quite serious. However, it's not untreatable and we'll fight it together.

患者：先生、私の病状はどれくらい深刻ですか?

医者：正直言って、かなり深刻です。ただし、治療不可能なわけではありませんし、一緒に戦いましょう。

B. The doctor admitted to the patient that his condition was serious but assured him it was treatable.

医者は患者に、彼の病状は深刻だが治療可能であると確信させました。

5. 🔊 u1205

Reporter: Minister, how does the government plan to handle the current crisis?

Minister: We have a comprehensive plan in place, and we are confident that we will navigate through these challenging times.

記者：大臣、政府は現在の危機にどのように対処する予定ですか?

大臣：全面的な計画が進行中であり、この厳しい時期を乗り越えることができると自信を持っています。

C. The Minister assured the reporter that he had a comprehensive plan to handle the crisis.

大臣は記者に、危機に対処するための包括的な計画があると確信させました。

6. 🔊 u1206

Fan: Ms. Roberts, did you enjoy working with the director, Mr. Anderson?

Ms. Roberts: It was a wonderful experience. I've learned so much from him.

ファン：アンダーソン監督との仕事は楽しかったですか、ロバーツさん?

ロバーツ氏：素晴らしい経験でした。監督からたくさんのことを学びました。

A. Ms. Roberts reported that working with director Anderson was a wonderful experience from which she learned a lot.

ロバーツ氏は、アンダーソン監督との仕事が素晴らしい経験であり、多くを学んだと報告しました。

Unit 13　間接話法 ②

Task 1

1.

Quote from Einstein: "The speed of light is independent of the motion of the observer."

アインシュタインの言葉：" 光の速度は観測者の運動に依存しない "

Indirect: Einstein, in his special theory of relativity, (B) **concludes** that the speed of light is independent of the motion of the observer.

間接：アインシュタインは彼の特殊相対性理論において、観測者の運動に関係なく光の速度は一定であると結論づけています。

2.

Quote from a business analyst: "Despite positive quarterly results, the company may not be able to sustain its growth rate."

ビジネスアナリストの言葉：" ポジティブな四半期結果にも関わらず、会社はその成長率を維持できないかもしれません "

Indirect: The business analyst (B) **questioned** the company's growth sustainability.

間接：ビジネスアナリストは、企業の成長の持続可能性に疑問を呈しました。

3.

Quote from Stephen Hawking: "One can't predict the future."

スティーブン・ホーキングの言葉：" 未来は予測できません "

Indirect: Stephen Hawking (C) **questioned** the predictability of the future.

間接：スティーブン・ホーキングは未来の予測可能性に疑問を呈しました。

4.

Quote from an environmental scientist: "We must take immediate action to reduce carbon emissions."

環境科学者の言葉：" 炭素排出量を削減するためにただちに行動を取る必要があります "

Indirect: The environmental scientist **(B) confirmed** the need for immediate action.

間接：環境科学者は即時の行動の必要性を確認しました。

5.

Quote from a corporate report: "The company has significantly increased its profits over the last fiscal year."

企業報告書からの引用：" 会社は昨年度に利益を大幅に増加させました "

Indirect: The corporate report **(C) notes** the company's increased profits.

間接：企業報告書は会社の利益増加に言及しています。

6.

Quote from Dr. Haller: "The results of the experiment are inconclusive."

ホーラー博士の言葉：" 実験の結果は決定的ではありません "

Indirect: Dr. Haller **(D) takes issue with** the experiment results.

間接：ホーラー博士は実験結果に問題があると指摘しています。

7.

Quote from Professor Smith: "The world is experiencing a digital revolution."

スミス教授の言葉：" 世界はデジタル革命を経験しています "

Indirect: Professor Smith **(B) observed** what he calls "a digital revolution".

間接：スミス教授は「デジタル革命」と呼ばれる現象を観察しました。

8.

Quote from a book critic: "The book's plot is highly improbable."

本の評論家の言葉：" 本のプロットは非常に現実味がない "

Indirect: The book critic **(C) takes issue with** the plot of the book.

間接：本の評論家は本のプロットに問題があると指摘しています。

9.

Quote from a technology expert: "AI is transforming every industry."

テクノロジー専門家の言葉："AI はすべての産業を変革しています "

Indirect: The technology expert (C) **acknowledges** the impact of AI.

間接：テクノロジー専門家は AI の影響を認識しています。

10.

Quote from an economist: "There's a direct correlation between education and income."

経済学者の言葉："教育と収入の間には直接的な相関関係があります "

Indirect: The economist (B) **affirms** a link between education and income.

間接：経済学者は教育と収入との相関関係を確認しています。

11.

Quote from a climate scientist: "The warming trend observed over the past few decades is likely due to human activity."

気候科学者の言葉："過去数十年間に観察された温暖化のトレンドは、おそらく人間の活動が原因です "

Indirect: The climate scientist (B) **contends** that human activity is the cause of the recent warming trend.

間接：気候科学者は、最近の温暖化トレンドの原因は人間の活動であると主張しています。

12.

Quote from a CEO: "Our company is committed to sustainable practices."

CEO の言葉："当社は持続可能な実践にコミットしています "

Indirect: The CEO (B) **expressed** the company's commitment to sustainable practices.

間接：CEO は企業の持続可能な実践へのコミットメントを表明しました。

1. 🔊 u1301

Sarah: How did the presentation go, John?

John: It went well. I believe our proposal was well received.

What does John mean?

サラ：ジョン、プレゼンテーションはどうだったの?

ジョン：上手くいったよ。私たちの提案は好意的に受け入れられたと思う。

ジョンの言いたいことは何ですか?

D. John indicated that the proposal was well received.

ジョンは提案が好意的に受け入れられたと示しています。

2. 🔊 u1302

Professor Carter: What do you think of the new physics theory, Amanda?

Amanda: To be honest, I think there are many holes in it.

What does Amanda mean?

カーター教授：新しい物理理論についてどう思いますか、アマンダ?

アマンダ：正直言って、多くの欠点があると思います。

アマンダの言いたいことは何ですか?

B. Amanda called into question the new physics theory.

アマンダは新しい物理理論に多くの欠点があると指摘しています。

3. 🔊 u1303

CEO: Have you considered my offer, Claire?

Claire: Yes, Thomas, and I am inclined to accept it.

What does Claire mean?

社長：クレア、私の提案を考えましたか?

クレア：はい、トーマス、お受けしたいと思っています。

クレアの言いたいことは何ですか?

C. Claire stated that she is likely to accept the offer made by Thomas.

クレアはトーマスからの提案を受け入れる可能性が高いと言っています。

4. 🔊 u1304

Mia: Are we going to the concert this weekend, Alex?

Alex: I don't think we should. The reviews for the band's performances have been pretty bad.

What does Alex mean?

Mia：今週末、コンサートに行くの、アレックス?

Alex：やめておいたほうが良いと思う。バンドのパフォーマンスのレビューがかなり悪かったから。

アレックスの言いたいことは何ですか?

C. Alex suggested that they shouldn't go to the concert.

アレックスはコンサートには行かないほうが良いと言っています。

5. 🔊 u1305

Dr. Kelly: How do you find the new lab equipment, Luke?

Luke: It's fantastic! I've never had an easier time with my experiments.

What does Luke mean?

ケリー博士：新しいラボ設備はどうだった、ルーク?

ルーク：素晴らしいです! こんなに実験が楽だったことはありません。

ルークの言いたいことは何ですか?

B. Luke acknowledges that the new lab equipment is great.

ルークは新しいラボ設備が素晴らしいと認めています。

6. 🔊 u1306

Adam: Did you find the new training helpful, Emma?

Emma: Not particularly. It felt like a lot of information with no clear guidance.

What does Emma mean?

アダム：新しいトレーニングは役に立ったか、エマ?

エマ：それほどではありません。情報が多いわりに、わかりやすい指導がなかった感じです。

エマの言いたいことは何ですか?

B. Emma challenged the effectiveness of the new training.

エマは新しいトレーニングの効果を疑問視しています。

7. 🔊 u1307

Paula: Are you enjoying the new art program, Oliver?

Oliver: Yes, very much! It's really helped me improve my skills.

What does Oliver mean?

ポーラ：新しいアートプログラムは楽しいですか、オリバー？

オリバー：はい、とても! 私のスキルが本当に向上しています。

オリバーの言いたいことは何ですか？

B. Oliver credited the art program with improving his skills.

オリバーはアートプログラムが彼のスキルを向上させたと信じています。

8. 🔊 u1308

George: How are you coping with the new training regimen, Lily?

Lily: It's hard, but I can see how it will make me a better athlete.

What does Lily mean?

ジョージ：新しいトレーニングプログラムはどうですか、リリー？

リリー：きついですが、それが私をより良い選手にするのがわかります。

リリーの言いたいことは何ですか？

B. Lily admitted that the training regimen is difficult but beneficial.

リリーはトレーニングプログラムが困難だが有益だと認識しています。

9. 🔊 u1309

Hannah: Have you tried the new menu at our cafeteria, David?

David: Yes, I have. It's not really to my liking.

What does David mean?

ハナ：カフェテリアの新しいメニューは食べてみた、デイビッド？

デイビッド：食べてみたよ。でも、あまり好きではないなあ。

デイビッドの言いたいことは何ですか？

B. David expresses his dislike of the new menu.

デイビッドは新しいメニューは好みではないと言っています。

10. 🔊 u1310

Nicole: What's your stance on the new climate policy, Senator Graham?

Senator Graham: I firmly believe it's a step in the right direction.

What does Senator Graham mean?

ニコール：新しい気候政策に対してはどのような立場ですか、グラハム議員？

グレイアム代議士：それが正しい方向への一歩だと固く信じています。

グレイアム議員は何を意味していますか？

C. Senator Graham supports the new climate policy.

グレイアム議員は新しい気候政策を支持しています。

Unit 14　数字と図表の表現

──────── Task 1 ────────

Jack ④　Lucy ①　Alex ③

🔊 u1401

Lucy: I'm a bit worried about the sudden drop we experienced in April. What do you think, Jack?

Jack: I see where you're coming from, Lucy, but it's not a big deal, trust me. Since we changed the user interface, there has been a steady climb in customer satisfaction, as you can see. What's your take, Alex?

Alex: I'm with Jack on this one. Our costs haven't really gone up, but since the user interface change we're seeing a surge in sales. Even the figures for April you're so worried about are not that bad.

ルーシー：4月に急激に減少したのが少し心配です。どう思いますか、ジャック？

ジャック：ルーシーの気持ちもわかりますが、大した問題ではありません、本当に。ユーザーインターフェイスを変更してから、顧客満足度が着実に上昇しているのがわかりますよね。アレックスはどう思いますか？

アレックス：この点に関してはジャックと同意見です。コストは実際には上がっていませんが、ユーザーインターフェイスの変更以降、販売が急増しています。心配している 4 月の数字もそんなに悪くないですよ。

(Task 2)

🔊 u1402

In addition to the issues we discussed, there are two more items I'd like to draw your attention to. First, (1) c. **temperature control**. During the hot months, we tend to believe that the cooler we make the place, the longer people will hang out, and (2) A. **therefore**, the more they'll buy from the various shops on each floor. However, that's not always the case. The data we took clearly (3) B. **indicate** that if it is too hot, customers spend only the minimum amount of time in-store. As counter-intuitive as it may be, the same data demonstrate that (4) D. **lowering** the temperature too much during the hot months drives customer away just as much. 25-26 degrees is apparently the (5) A. **optimal** summer temperature. At 22 degrees, there is a (6) B. **sharp decline** in the time they spend with us. Similarly, at 30 degrees it (7) B. **declines by more than half**.

Another item on the agenda is what kind of tenant we should look for to fill in the vacancy on the 4th floor. I found some data from other department stores, and based on these data, I believe we should rethink our original idea to let the space to a gallery. The data represent the (8) D. **percentage** of customers who came to visit one specific store but also ended up making unplanned purchases from other stores. Needless to say, we want the customers to purchase from multiple stores. In that respect, renting to a café is by far the best option, in my opinion. If we have a café on the 4th floor we can practically (9) A. **double** the cross-merchandising effect.

話し合った問題に加えて、注目すべき 2 つの項目があります。まず、温度管理です。暑い間は、場所を涼しくすればするほど、人々が長く滞在すると信じがちです。したがって、各階のさまざまな店舗からもっ

と買ってもらえると考えます。しかし、必ずしもそうとは限りません。私たちが取ったデータは、店内があまりにも暑いと、顧客は必要最低限の時間しか店内に滞在しないことを明確に示しています。直感に反するかもしれませんが、暑い月に温度を下げすぎると、顧客を同じくらい遠ざけることが、同じデータで示されています。25〜26度が最適な夏の温度のようです。22度では、彼らが私たちと過ごす時間が急激に減少します。同様に、30度では半分以下になります。

別の項目は、4階の空きスペースを埋めるためにどのようなテナントを探すべきかということです。私は他のデパートからのデータを見つけましたが、これらのデータに基づいて、スペースをギャラリーに貸し出すという当初のアイデアを見直すべきだと考えています。データは、特定の店を訪れたが、他の店からも予定外の買い物をした顧客の割合を表しています。言うまでもなく、私たちが願うのは、顧客が複数の店から購入することです。その点を考慮すると、私の意見では、カフェを検討するのが最善の選択です。4階にカフェがあれば、クロスマーチャンダイジング効果を実質的に2倍にすることができます。

Unit 15 総仕上げ問題

【1】

1. (A) **Owing to** the heavy rain, the school event has been postponed.
    激しい雨のため、学校のイベントが延期されました。

2. One of the (B) **benefits** of online learning is the flexibility it offers.
    オンライン学習の利点の一つは、柔軟性があることです。

3. Smoking (B) **leads to** numerous health problems, including heart disease.
    喫煙は、心臓病を含め、数多くの健康問題を引き起こします。

4. The recent policy change can be (A) **attributed to** the efforts of the community activists.
    最近の政策変更は地域社会活動家の努力が実を結んだものと言えそうです。

5. One (D) **merit** of living in the city is the easy access to public transportation.
    都市での生活の利点の一つは、公共交通機関への簡単なアクセスです。

6. The rise in temperatures (A) **was caused by** an increase in forest fires in the region.

   一帯の気温の上昇は森林火災の増加によって引き起こされました。

7. The (C) **disadvantage** of this strategy is that it may alienate some long-term customers.

   この戦略のデメリットは、長年の顧客の一部を疎外する可能性があることです。

8. The new feature has been welcomed by users (A) **thanks to** its user-friendliness.

   新機能は、その使いやすさのおかげでユーザーから歓迎されました。

9. (C) **Owing to** rigorous training, the team was able to achieve a resounding victory.

   厳しいトレーニングのおかげで、チームは華々しい勝利を達成できました。

10. The (B) **positive effect** of using renewable energy sources is that they can reduce the carbon footprint significantly.

   再生可能エネルギー源を使用する利点は、カーボンフットプリントを大幅に削減できることです。

11. Increased water pollution (D) **can be attributed to** the dumping of industrial waste in the river.

   水質汚染の増加は、川への産業廃棄物の投棄が原因と言えます。

12. Insufficient rainfall will (C) **produce** a significant decrease in crop yields, affecting the livelihoods of many farmers.

   降水量が不足すると、作物の収量が大幅に減少し、多くの農民の生計に影響を与えます。

13. The decision to work remotely has its (C) **pros and cons**, such as decreased commuting time, and fewer opportunities for communication with coworkers.

リモートで働く決定には、通勤時間短縮の一方で同僚とのコミュニケーション機会の減少といった、長所と短所があります。

14. (B) **Due to** the lack of evidence, the theory cannot be accepted as true.

証拠が不足しているため、この理論は真実として受け入れることができません。

15. The (A) **advantage** of this material is its high resistance to heat and chemicals.

この素材の利点は、高い耐熱性と化学薬品耐性です。

【B】

1. Until 1962, St Paul's Cathedral had been (B) **London's tallest** building for over 250 years.

1962 年まで、セントポール大聖堂は 250 年以上にわたってロンドンで最も高い建物でした。

2. If I were (D) **as strong as** my brother, I would be a wrestler too.

もし私が兄と同じくらい強ければ、私もレスラーになるだろう。

3. The United States is (C) **significantly larger** than Germany.

アメリカ合衆国は、ドイツよりかなり大きいです。

4. The likelihood of experiencing snow is (B) **much higher** if you go there in January.

1 月に行った方が雪を体験できる可能性がより高いです。

5. Having (A) **a narrower focus** is important if you want to succeed in business.

ビジネスで成功するには、より絞った焦点を持つことが重要です。

6. Everyone thought that Jane had the (C) **stronger** argument.
ジェーンの論点がより優れていると全員が思いました。

7. This book helped me gain a (D) **deeper** understanding of epistemology.
この本は私が認識論のより深い理解を得る助けとなりました。

8. Gamers typically look for (B) **faster** computers and bigger monitors.
ゲーマーは、通常、より速いパソコンとより大きなモニターを求めます。

9. To become an Olympic champion, you need to run at least (C) **slightly faster** than the second guy.
オリンピックチャンピオンになるには、二位の人より少なくとも少し速く走らなければなりません。

10. My (B) **best** friend Brian is getting married on Saturday.
親友のブライアンが土曜日に結婚します。

【C】

1.

1. **If** you decide to come to the party, please let me know.
もしパーティーに来ることにしたら、教えてください。

2. I will call you **when** I arrive at the airport.
空港に到着したら、（あなたに）電話します。

3. She will be very happy **when** she receives your gift.
彼女はあなたのプレゼントを受け取ったらとても喜びます。

4. **If** it rains tomorrow, we will have to cancel the picnic.
明日雨が降ったら、ピクニックをキャンセルしなければなりません。

5. They will announce their decision **when** the meeting concludes.
会議が終わったら、彼らはその決定を発表します。

6. **When** you you're next in Tokyo, don't forget to try the sushi at the Tsukiji market.

次回東京に来た際には、築地市場の寿司を食べてみるのを忘れないでください。

7. **If** we don't receive the shipment by Friday, we will contact the supplier.

金曜日までに荷物が届かない場合、サプライヤーに連絡します。

8. I will send you the report **when** I finish it.

レポートを書き終えたら、（あなたに）送ります。

9. **If** you fail the exam, ask the teacher for help.

試験に不合格になった場合、先生に助けを求めてください。

10. We will go for a hike **if** the weather is nice this weekend.

今週末天気が良ければ、ハイキングに行きます。

解答・訳・解説

2.

1. He would be an expert in Japanese (B) **if** he practiced daily for years.

彼が何年もの間、毎日練習していたら、日本語の専門家になっていたでしょう。

2. She would have succeeded if she (C) **had worked** harder.

もっと一生懸命に働いていたら、彼女は成功していたでしょう。

3. I would be happier if he (B) **visited** more often.

彼がもっと頻繁に来てくれたらいいのに（私はもっと幸せだろうに）。

4. If it (C) **doesn't rain** tomorrow, we will have a picnic.

明日雨が降らなければ、ピクニックに行きます。

5. They would be here by now (B) **if** they had caught the early train.

早い電車に乗っていたら、彼らは今ここにいたでしょう。

6. She wishes she (C) **had learned** the piano as a child.

彼女は子供の頃にピアノを習っておけば良かったと思っています。

7. If you (C) **tell** the truth, I will forgive you.

本当のことを言えば許してあげる（あなたが真実を言えば、私はあなたを許します）。

8. They could have visited the museum if they (D) **had arrived** earlier.

もっと早く到着していたら、彼らは博物館に行けたのに。

9. She would have felt better (B) **if** she had taken her medicine.

薬を飲んでいたら彼女は具合が良くなっていたのに。

10. You would have known the answer (C) **had** you paid attention in class.

授業中に注意を払っていたら、答えがわかったのにね。

11. I will lend you the money, (B) **provided** you pay me back by the end of the month.

月末までに返してくれるのならお金を貸します。

12. If she (C) **had gone** to the concert, she would have met the singer.

コンサートに行っていたら、彼女はその歌手に会えたでしょう。

13. I wish I (C) **had** more time to spend with my family.

もっと家族と過ごす時間があればなあ。

14. He will finish the project on time if he (A) **starts** now.

彼が今始めれば、プロジェクトは時間通りに終わるでしょう。

15. I wish I (D) **had told** her when I had the chance.

チャンスがあったときに彼女に言っていたらなあ。

【D】

1. We visited several museums in the city, (A) **for example** the Natural History Museum and the art gallery.

   私たちは市内のいくつかの博物館を訪れました。たとえば、自然史博物館や美術館です。

2. I believe the project will be a success; (B) **moreover**, it has the backing of several prominent industry leaders.

   プロジェクトが成功すると私は信じています。それに、いくつかの有名な業界リーダーの支援を受けてもいます。

3. The scientist made a significant discovery; (D) **namely**, he found a way to improve the efficiency of solar panels by 20%.

   その科学者は重要な発見をしました。すなわち、太陽電池の効率を 20%向上させる方法を見つけました。

4. The trip was not only educational but (A) **also** fun and exciting.

   その旅行は教育的だけでなく、楽しくてわくわくするものでもありました。

5. This Japanese company has been rapidly expanding throughout Asia. (B) **Furthermore**, the company plans to expand its operations to European markets in the coming years.

   この日本企業はアジア中に素早く展開しています。さらに、その企業は今後数年間でヨーロッパ市場への事業拡大を計画しています。

6. The documentary was extremely informative; it covered various topics, (A) **such as** climate change and conservation efforts.

   そのドキュメンタリーは非常に情報満載でした。気候変動や保全努力など、さまざまなトピックを取り上げていました。

7. The artist's performance at the concert was incredible. (B) **Furthermore,** the lighting and sound system were top-notch.

   コンサートは信じられないほど素晴らしかったです。さらに、照明とサウンドシステムが最高でした。

8. He is a talented musician, playing instruments (B) **such as** guitar, piano, and drums.

   彼は才能ある音楽家で、ギターやピアノ、ドラムなどの楽器を演奏します。

9. She helped organize the potluck, brought games for everyone, and played the piano. (D) **In addition**, she also brought a homemade apple pie.

   彼女は持ち寄り料理のパーティーの企画を手伝い、皆のためのゲームを持ってきて、ピアノも弾いてくれました。さらに、手作りのアップルパイも持ってきました。

10. The book covers a lot of complex theories; (A) **on top of that**, it includes a section on quantum physics.

    その本は多くの複雑な理論を取り上げています。その上、量子物理学のセクションも含まれています。

11. The new mall has a wide range of stores, (D) **in other words** a cinema and a large food court.

    新しいモールにはさまざまな店があります。それには映画館や大きなフードコートも含まれます。

12. The report outlined several potential solutions, (C) **including** increasing funding for public transportation.

    その報告書はいくつかの潜在的な解決策を概説しており、公共交通機関への資金提供の増加も含まれています。

13. I know you want to see it, so I won't reveal much. (A) **In a nutshell**, the movie was both thrilling and thought-provoking.

    見に行きたいと思うだろうから、あまりたくさん言わないでおきますね。要するに、その映画はスリリングで、かつ考えさせられるものでした。

14. I have visited several countries in Europe, (C) **such as** France, Italy, and Germany.

    私はヨーロッパのいくつかの国を訪れました。たとえばフランス、イタリア、ドイツなどです。

15. The artist is known for his unique style; (B) **Namely**, his paintings often feature vibrant colors and abstract shapes.

そのアーティストは独特のスタイルで知られています。すなわち、彼の絵はしばしば鮮やかな色と抽象的な形を特徴としています。

16. The show was excellent. (A) **In particular**, the lead actor delivered a phenomenal performance.

ショーは素晴らしかったです。とりわけ、主演俳優は素晴らしい演技でした。

17. The novel had a very interesting plot; (D) **furthermore**, it gave deep insights into the human psyche.

その小説はとても面白いストーリーでした。さらに、人間の心理に深い洞察を提供していました。

18. He is an expert in many areas of science, (A) **including** physics and chemistry.

彼は、物理学と化学も含め、科学の多くの分野で専門家です。

19. They decided to renovate the entire house; (C) **in addition**, they plan to add a new garden.

彼らは家全体を改装することにしました。さらに、新しい庭を追加する予定です。

20. The technology is innovative and, (B) **what's more**, it has the potential to revolutionize the whole industry.

その技術は革新的であり、さらに、業界全体に大変革をもたらす可能性があります。

【E】

1. He had a minor accident in the morning; (D) **nevertheless**, he managed to arrive at the meeting on time.

彼は朝軽い事故に遭いましたが、それでもなんとか会議には時間通り到着しました。

2. She is very good at playing the piano; (A) **however**, she cannot play the violin.

   彼女はピアノを弾くのが非常に上手です、しかし、バイオリンは弾けません。

3. The Northern region experiences cold and snowy winters, (A) **in contrast**, the Southern region enjoys warm and sunny weather.

   北部では冬は寒く雪が降りますが、それに対して、南部は暖かく晴れた気候です。

4. She had all the qualifications for the job; (A) **still**, she wasn't selected.

   彼女はその仕事の資格をすべて持っていましたが、それでも選ばれませんでした。

5. He is known for his calm demeanor, (C) **whereas** his sister is quite impulsive.

   彼は冷静な態度で知られていますが、それに対して彼の姉はかなり衝動的です。

6. Many people recommended the movie, (B) **yet** I didn't enjoy it very much.

   多くの人がその映画を勧めていましたが、それでも私はあまり楽しめませんでした。

7. He still makes time to mentor new employees, (A) **even though** he has a very important role in the company.

   彼は会社で非常に重要な役割を担っていますが、それでも新入社員の指導をする時間は作っています。

8. (A) **Regardless of** the rain, they decided to go ahead with the picnic.

   雨にもかかわらず、彼らはピクニックを強行することにしました。

9. He doesn't like sweets; (D) **nevertheless** he ate the piece of cake so as not to offend the host.

   彼は甘いものが好きではありませんが、とは言ってもホストを怒らせないように出されたケーキを食べました。

10. She doesn't enjoy going to the gym, (B) **although** she goes there every day to maintain her health.

彼女はジムに行くのが好きではないですが、それでも健康を維持するために毎日通っています。

【F】

（※あくまで解答例です）

A bicycle is a vehicle used for transportation on roads and paths.

自転車は、道路や小道での輸送に使用される乗り物です。

A bakery is a place where bread and other baked goods are made and sold.

ベーカリーは、パンや他の焼き菓子が作られて販売される場所です。

A balcony is a structure protruding from the side of a building.

バルコニーは、建物の側面から突き出た構造です。

A battery is a device used to store electrical energy for later use.

電池は、後で使う電気エネルギーを保存するためのデバイスです。

A brochure is a document used to provide information or to promote something, usually in a concise printed format.

ブロシュアは、情報を提供したり何かを宣伝したりするための文書で、通常は簡潔な印刷形式のものです。

A cafeteria is a place where food is provided in a self-service manner, often found in schools or office buildings.

カフェテリアは、学校やオフィスビルによくある、セルフサービス方式で食事が提供される場所です。

A calendar is a system used to organize and measure time, often in terms of days, months, and years.

暦は、通常は日、月、年という単位で時間を整理し計測するためのシステムです。

【G】

1.

Mike: "I didn't take your phone, I swear!"

Jane: "I'm not sure I believe you."

Jane (A) **expressed** doubt towards Mike's words.

マイク：君の電話を持って行ってないよ、ほんとだってば!

ジェーン：あなたを信じるかどうかわからない。

ジェーンはマイクの言葉に対して疑念を示しました。

2.

Anna: "I am sure the event will be cancelled due to the storm."

Ben: "That's not true; the organizers said it would continue as planned."

Ben (B) **rebutted** Anna's statement.

アンナ：嵐のせいでイベントはきっと中止になるわね。

ベン：そんなことないよ。主催者は計画通りに進行すると言っていた。

ベンはアンナの発言に反論しました。

3.

Trisha: "The meeting will start at 10 am, not a minute later."

Oliver: "Actually, the email says it will start at 10:30 am."

Oliver (C) **corrected** Trisha's information.

トリシャ：ミーティングは午前 10 時に始まります、1 分たりとも遅れることはありません。

オリバー：実は、メールには 10 時 30 分開始と書いてあります。

オリバーはトリシャの情報を訂正しました。

4.

Sarah: "I will never be able to complete this project on time."

Kevin: "I know you can do it, just believe in yourself."

Kevin (B) **dismissed** Sarah's pessimism.

サラ：私はこのプロジェクトを期限内に終えることはできないと思う。

ケビン：君ならできる、自分を信じて。

ケビンはサラの悲観主義をはねつけました。

5.

David: "I promise, I'll repay the loan within a month."

Rita: "You better, I am counting on your word."

Rita **(B) believed** in David's promise.

デイビッド：約束するよ、お金は 1 ヶ月以内に返す。

リタ：そうしてくれると嬉しいわ、あなたの言葉を信じているから。

リタはデイビッドの約束を信じました。

【H】

1. In the middle of the heatwave, the sale of air conditioners **(B) soared**.

    猛暑の真っ只中で、エアコンの売り上げが急増しました。

2. After the severe storm, the number of tourists in the seaside town **(C) decreased** dramatically.

    厳しい嵐の後、海辺の町の観光客の数が劇的に減少しました。

3. Due to the introduction of new technology, the company's production capacity **(A) surged** in the last year.

    新技術の導入により、昨年は会社の生産能力が急増しました。

4. The announcement of tax increases negatively affected investor sentiment, and the stock market **(C) plummeted**.

    増税の発表は投資家心理にネガティブに作用し、株式市場は急落しました。

5. Despite the economic recovery, the unemployment rate has **(C) remained stable** over the past few months.

    経済の回復にもかかわらず、失業率は過去数ヶ月間安定していました。

6. Due to better healthcare facilities, the average lifespan in the country has **(A) expanded** in the past decade.

    医療施設が改善された影響で、過去 10 年間で国の平均寿命は伸びました。

7. Following the negative reviews, the sales of the product (D) **plummeted**.

批判的なレビューを受けて、製品の販売は急落しました。

8. Due to an improved marketing strategy, the brand's popularity has (C) **soared** in recent years.

マーケティング戦略を改善した結果、ブランドの人気は近年急激に高まりました。

9 After several years of drought, the lake's water level (C) **dropped** significantly.

数年間の干ばつの後、湖の水位が著しく低下しました。

10. Following a successful advertising campaign, the company's market share (B) **expanded** in a short period.

実りある広告キャンペーンを受け、会社の市場シェアは短期間で拡大しました。

著者紹介

コチェフ アレクサンダー（Alexander Kotchev）

株式会社オレンジバード執行役員 COO。北海道大学法学部卒業後、広告会社勤務のかたわらフリーランス翻訳者として活動。2009 年より現職。主に高校生以上を対象に、留学準備、TOEFL・IELTS をはじめとした検定対策、自立した英語話者の育成を専門とする英語研修を提供している。
著書は、『完全攻略！TOEFL iBT テスト リーディング リスニング』、『完全攻略！TOEFL iBT テスト スピーキング ライティング』、『完全攻略！IELTS 英単語 3500』（すべてアルク刊）。
他に、IIBC 刊の『公式 TOEIC Listening & Reading プラクティス リーディング編』並びに『公式 TOEIC Listening& Reading プラクティスリスニング編』をはじめとして、15 冊以上の教材の編集に携わる。
興味ある分野は、第二言語習得全般、語彙、TOEFL や IELTS などの検定やテスト設計。

◉── 校正　　　　　　　　　　Eleanor Clark, Ph.D.、飯田了子
◉── 付属音声ナレーション　　Diana Shugarman、Steven Toth
◉── 録音・編集　　　　　　　株式会社 STUDIO RICCIO
◉── カバーデザイン　　　　　松本 聖典
◉── DTP・本文図版　　　　　スタジオ・ポストエイジ

［音声 DL 付］意見・主張をクリアに伝える技術 ディスコースマーカーで英語はこんなに伝わる

2023 年 10 月 25 日　　　　初版発行

著者	コチェフ アレクサンダー
発行者	内田 真介
発行・発売	ベレ出版 〒162-0832　東京都新宿区岩戸町12 レベッカビル TEL.03-5225-4790 FAX.03-5225-4795 ホームページ　https://www.beret.co.jp/
印刷	三松堂株式会社
製本	根本製本株式会社

ISBN 978-4-86064-742-1 C2082　　　　　　　　　　　編集担当　大石裕子

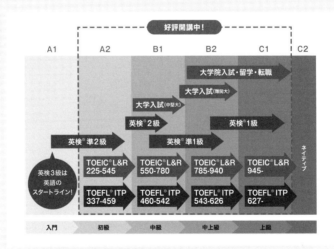